THE MYSTERY WRITER'S HANDBOOK
Newly Revised Edition

MYSTERY WRITER'S

HANDBOOK

by The Mystery Writers of America
newly revised edition

Writer's Digest
9933 Alliance Road • Cincinnati, Ohio 45242

Library of Congress Cataloguing in Publication Data

Mystery Writers of America
The mystery writer's handbook
1. Detective and mystery stories—Technique
I. Title
PN3377.5.D4M9 1975 808.3'872 75-33828
ISBN 0-911654-41-0

Writer's Digest
Div., F&W Publishing Corporation
9933 Alliance Road
Cincinnati, Ohio 45242

To the hundreds
of MWA members
who have contributed
time, talent and faith

Contents

PART I: THE WRITER

Members of the Mystery Writers of America were sent questionnaires to determine their methods and preferences in writing. Why do they prefer to write? "I like to," "It's my life," "I have a storyteller's compulsion" are but a few of the answers.

The gothic is storytelling at its most exciting. And at its most profitable. Where to set the story, how to handle sex, and how to build suspense are matters taken up here by an expert.

To the publishing industry, softcover books are for the same audience that's hooked on TV. That means the books must have some of TV's more obvious qualities, such as lots of action and scenes bristling with dialogue.

Short stories are not novels that just never grew up. They are time-tested ideals, this author explains, for the puzzle-and-resolution yarn. Some good advice on how to use the form well.

There's a wide-open market for the true crime story. So it's one of the easier types for a beginner to break in. It's not so easy, however, to do the detailed research involved and then weave the facts into a gripping narrative.

Preface

One afternoon a few years ago I happened to meet a Hungarian writer who was a friend of mine, and we sat down in the nearest cafeteria for a cup of coffee. He asked me what I was doing and where I was going, and I told him I was on my way to MWA headquarters to teach a class in writing.

He stared in disbelief. "You're joking," he said.

"No. What's funny about teaching?"

"You're really going out to create competion?" he said. Then the slow, sly grin of a born con man crossed his face. "I know." he said." "You teach them the wrong thing."

The members of the Mystery Writers of America, however, believe in competition, and believe that it keeps raising the standards in their field. The mystery demands a disciplined talent and a greater sense of form than do other types of the novel. The tradition of Edgar Allan Poe and Arthur Conan Doyle may have languished for a while, but with the advent of Dashiell Hammett it flared up and reached the golden age of mystery writing.

The specifics of this book are guidelines which are

beyond price, but they are intended to be guidelines only. You will find writers contradicting each other on methods and approaches to their craft. This is all to the good, for a writer is not the product of a machine that stamps out an endless parade of duplicates. In the pages of this book you will not find rigid laws that you are instructed to follow to fame and glory. Rather, you will find suggestions from which to select. The value of *The Handbook* is that it presents a wide variety of writing methods, all of which have been tried and proven by successful pros. A fellow writer once told me he'd rather dig ditches than follow my particular methods. I returned the compliment.

You will find short-cuts, hints, and clues that will save you months, if not years, of trial and error, although in the end you will plod you own path, for there are no universal rules and regulations for the creation of a writer. You will struggle and hope, and either you end up making a living out of it, or else you don't. But either way, your life will be enriched. And after studying this volume, you will read more critically and with a greater appreciation. Your own observation should grow keener, you'll learn something of the art of the story teller, which is what writers are and always have been, throughout the thousands of years since the time when the first writers scratched out their laborious cuneiform on wet clay tablets.

Although this is a volume by mystery writers on mystery writing, it transcends the field. All writers in all genres, short story writers and novelists, article writers and non-fiction writers, will find advice and information on such matters as style, dialogue, how to create character, and how to revise, as well as a symposium on subjects such as working methods and how to overcome writing blocks. Even the non-writer will be fascinated and amazed by the insights and experiences that thread through these pages. In a real sense you will walk into a writer's study, where you can either learn, or else just sit down and watch.

The essential home-reference shelf of every writer starts with a dictionary, preferably unabridged, and a thesaurus. The mystery writer also needs up to date editions of texts on criminal investigation, such as Soderman and O'Connell's *Modern Criminal Investigation;* on forensic medicine, such as Gonzales, Vance, Helpern and Umberger's *Legal Medicine, Pathology and Toxicology;* and on police science, such as O'Hara and Osterburg's *Introduction to Criminalistics.*

There is a vast amount of useful literature covering different aspects of the crime field — law, forensic medicine, ballistics, fingerprint and voice identification, and so on — and new scientific methods are developed every year. It is suggested that you go to your local library and pick out what best suits your needs. But the purpose of this book is to help you to become a writer, and to understand writers and writing, as exemplified by that fundamental and well-loved genre — the mystery story.

What, then, is a mystery story? The term has been thrown around loosely, but it derives from a classic form, which at the very least sets out a template that is a model of logical construction. Four elements fuse to form this structure. Let's call them the rules of the classic mystery.

Rule 1: There must be a crime and it must be personalized to the point where the reader cares. Usually, but not always, the crime is murder, since murder is the most serious crime known to man. The readers must want to see its solution, must want to see the criminal caught. If a troop of cowboys shoots up a town and happens to wing the town drunk, nobody cares particularly whether the marauders are caught. But if the shooting is intentional and the town drunk turns out to be a spy in disguise, or if the murderer is the unknown bandit with a pair of toucan bills in his hat, then the reader's interest is aroused and he longs to see justice done and the mystery solved.

Rule 2: The criminal must appear reasonably early in the story. Although one of the jobs of the author is to conceal the identity of the murderer from the reader, this does not give the author a license to introduce a totally new character on page 214 and reveal him as the murderer on page 215. The villain of the piece must be evident for a goodly portion of the book.

Rule 3: The author must be rigorously honest, and all clues, whether physical, such as a fingerprint, or a dropped purple bandanna, a character trait or an emotional relationship between people, must be made available to the reader. He is the alter ego of the protagonist, and the reader must know everything that the protagonist knows. Under no circumstances, for example, can Mr. Detective point to Mr. Killer and say, "you are the guilty party because you are lefthanded," unless somewhere in the story (cleverly concealed, of course) it has been established that only a lefthanded person could have killed Mr. Victim, and that Mr. Killer, and no one else, is lefthanded. In a similar manner, the dithery school teacher cannot be disclosed at the end of the story as the vicious spy unless somewhere along the line she's been revealed as a former actress or she shows herself capable of vicious, non-dithery behavior.

Rule 4: The detective must exert effort to catch the criminal, and the criminal must exert effort to fool the detective and escape from him. Coincidence is taboo. Sherlock Bones can't sit and think in his Leatherette armchair, while Moriarity holes up in comfort, until a passerby happens to notify Sherlock that there's a funny-looking guy down the street. Whereupon Sherlock stops thinking, Moriarity stops holing up, and Sherlock nabs Moriarity and then explains that he really expected this to happen all the time. While these are devices of the mystery story, they are the hallmarks of all story-telling. Translated into general terms, we can say that (1) the problem that faces the characters must be of sufficient importance to engage the reader's attention; (2) all vital characters should play their roles throughout; (3) coming events must cast their shadows before them; and (4) the characters must face their problems and do something about them.

These rules are inherent in the minds of the contributors to this book, which contains the concentrated wisdom and experience of the several hundred members of the Mystery Writers of America. Some of the names you will see are world famous, some are barely known, but all of them stand equal in exposing their methods, their bugaboos, their professional secrets. And no one in this book has received so much as a cent for the time and talent he has contributed.

Why do we do this? Basically because we respect our craft and honor its great tradition. We believe that the sense of form required in the mystery field tends to enhance good writing, and we believe that good writing is vital to the health of our culture and civilization. In the course of trying to tell stories, gracefully and creatively, it often happens that we weave our ideas and principles into the fabric of our writing. In a distant day, when people wonder what life was like in the twentieth century, they may research the forgotten books of mystery writers, and they will mine gold. They will find that the vast body of mystery writing reflects the contemporary scene as accurately and honestly as any *Comédie Humaine* could possibly do.

Ask any one of us why he writes, and he'll say he does it for a living, and usually not a luxurious living at that. But offer him a job that means an increase in his income, and he may walk away without even answering, for his love affair with his work is nothing that he can explain.

We write because we want to write, and in the course of it, we come to understand people and, perhaps, to be more honest and more compassionate with them and with ourselves. We are idealists and we are not idealists, which is a cryptic remark that can best be explained by reprinting

from the first edition of this book a quotation from an Anna
Mary Wells article:

> From generation to generation we need to be
> reminded that Shakespeare was never highbrow. He
> wrote plays designed to hit the popular taste and
> make money; he wrote them fast, and he succeeded
> in what he was trying to do. That they were also
> great plays, that he packed layer upon layer of
> meaning below the surface meaning, and that he
> carried the English language to its highest reaches
> of beauty and expressiveness — all of this is a divi-
> dend for posterity.
>
> *Hamlet* is a thundering good blood tragedy. It
> has all the gore, the plot complication, the horror,
> the ghosts and the low comedy that Elizabethan
> taste demanded and got in hundreds of other plays
> long since forgotten. Shakespeare did not consider
> himself too good for any of it.
>
> Did he know it was a great play? He knew it
> was a good one and a popular one, but beyond that
> was he aware of what he had accomplished? Perhaps
> at moments over a mug of ale in the Mermaid Tav-
> ern. Such moments are what all writers live for, and
> let us hope that he had his share of them.

May you, also, write stories of which you are proud.

An additional word: the earlier edition of this book was
planned and executed by the late Herbert Brean, who had
started to gather material for the present volume. In a real
sense I compiled this volume in collaboration with him, and
I'm sure he would join me in thanking the hundreds of MWA
members who answered questionnaires and contributed articles. Finally, I have relied heavily on the wisdom and advice
of the two other members of my committee, Hillary Waugh
and Richard Martin Stern.

— *Lawrence Treat*

1. Why Do You Write?

A questionnaire consisting of six questions was sent to all members of MWA. A selection from the hundreds of answers forms the backbone of this book, and my difficulty as an editor was in the threshing. There was plenty of wheat, but little chaff; and what was left out merely reinforces what you will find here.

The first question read as follows: Why, would you say, do you write, and especially why do you write mystery stories?

In other words, what kind of an animal is this *homo scribens*? What makes him tick, what does he think of his profession?

Although writers rarely agree on anything, answers to this question were almost unanimous.

BRUCE GRAEME states the case as tersely and succinctly as anyone could:

I write because writing is my life. When I cease writing, I shall die.

HARRY HARRISON says it less dramatically:

I write because I am a writer, and that is what makes life tick over. I work all the time; that is, everything I see, read or hear is applied to my work.

DOROTHY SALISBURY DAVIS says:

I cannot conceive of myself not writing — nor of myself not trying always to write better and deeper.

MIGNON G. EBERHART adds something, and reveals a bit of herself:

I write because I like to — sometimes hate it but have to write; started when very young, almost as soon as I could put pencil to paper.

COLLIN WILCOX echoes the same duality:

I've always considered writing an amiable vice — you can't help yourself, but it doesn't hurt much.

But sometimes it does hurt. LAWRENCE KAMARCK wonders:

Why do I write? Dear God! There's some sort of compulsion involved. I despise the physical act of writing, but I've conditioned myself to sit behind a typewriter for long periods of time, so the physical act becomes and is habit. I suppose I have a story-teller's compulsion. I want to tell somebody what's happening to all of us; I'm convinced nobody *really* knows but me. And because I want to keep the listener's attention, I tell my story with as much force and drama as possible, within credible limits.

JOSH PACHTER admits:

I hate the act of writing, but I love having written something.

ERIC AMBLER says modestly:

I write for a living and I write what I can.

LILLIAN DE LA TORRE gives a literary reference:

Like Boswell, I write because writing completes, clarifies, and enriches experience.

PAULINE SMITH tells us what so many other writers say, and goes on to romanticize:

I write because I must. I think in words. A writer has the advantage of leading a profligate life, robbing a bank, killing off his detractors and escaping from it all without ever leaving the typewriter. How else could I become, at the instant of an idea, a young-and-beautiful sexpot AND at the same time, a male-chauvinist-pig?

JOE GORES makes an interesting point:

I write to make a living, as a bricklayer lays bricks to make a living. I am a craftsman, working in words rather than mortar. Beyond that, in a larger sense, I write because I have a compulsion to write, to communicate, to tell stories. You are never in competition with other writers, only with yourself and with the material you are working with.

He then goes on to tell why he chose mystery stories, and his answer is echoed by about half of the others:

I write mystery stories because I enjoy reading them. All writers should write the sort of stories they like to read. No writer should ever forget, no matter how seriously he might take himself, that in an ultimate sense he is an entertainer, whether he wishes to be or not. *Hamlet* is moving, brooding, tragic — but also superb entertainment.

LILLIAN DE LA TORRE reflects the feelings of a number of writers when she says:

I write mystery stories because they provide a tight *form* within which to display the rich variety of life.

CLAYTON MATTHEWS agrees:

In my opinion, much of the fiction published today, both the short and long, is plotless, without form. To work, the mystery *must* have a beginning, middle and end.

MARY CRAIG brings together most of these reasons, and relates them to both the outer world and the inner world. She says:

For God's sake. I write because it is what I would
rather do than anything else in the world except
maybe play tennis (one does tire after three sets)
and play chess. (The opponent tires after two
games.) And because I have a compulsive sense of
order, an insatiable curiosity about motive, a genuine passion for words, and I like to take things in
a state of chaos and render them into something
intellectually or visually manageable. (I like to bake
bread for the same reason.) And I think people are
the only frontier left, really. Fifteen years ago I
might have mouthed some platitude about people
never changing, but the revolutions in thought and
mores in that period have lifted a curtain on a fascinating range of perspectives. I write mystery
stories because I like to read them, because it is
exhilarating to solve a puzzle backwards and because they, almost of a necessity, contain the factors
that bring human exposure: high stress situations
that break through the image projection that people
have planned and expose the nice Chaucerian warts
underneath.

DANA LYON gives us a frank and fascinating account of how she came to write first the straight
novel and then the mystery, which reverses the development of a number of other writers. She tells
us:

I started writing long ago at a time when there
weren't any psychiatrists—instead, I unburdened
myself at the typewriter. Seeing myself in print gave
me an ego trip that I couldn't get anywhere else,
and I wrote book after book (most of them published) without making any mark on the literary
world and with very little money to show for it. One
day I read a really miserable example of the hard-

boiled school of mystery and told myself, "Even I could do better than that," so I wrote one, a novella, and sold it. The dust jacket, in describing the contents, added "And watch Dana Lyon!" This did my ego no end of good, and it also inspired me to keep on with mysteries. It takes a specialty to get anyone anywhere!

MORRIS HERSHMAN is mundane and practical:

I have written mysteries because I was almost certain of an eventual sale in the short-story medium.

AARON MARC STEIN touches on the same practical reason, but adds something:

I write mysteries because once I began on them, I found I had a solid market there and also because I enjoy working with highly-structured stories (algebraic equations? Swiss watches?) and the highly-structured story line has fallen out of fashion in most other forms of the novel.

JOHN D. MACDONALD verbalizes what many writers feel about the mystery field:

I do not try to sort my books out into neat little boxes labeled 'mystery' or 'suspense' or 'straight novel.' I have no objection to others categorizing my work. It must give them some sense of security to have all the labels neatly attached. It would disturb them to find out how many labels are, in truth, interchangeable.

And finally ROSS MACDONALD reflects on his own reasons for writing mysteries:

Mystery stories have always interested me because they seem to correspond to life, especially inner life. They deal with the problems of causality and guilt that concern me.

Having found out what a writer is and why he writes and why he's chosen the mystery field, let's find out what the mystery story itself is. It turns out to be what used to be called a detective story. As it broadened, as writers developed the form and widened its perimeters, it came to be called the mystery novel, here in America. In England it went under the name of thriller or crime story. The truth of the matter is that these labels concern merchandising rather than some intrinsic characteristic peculiar to the so-called mystery novel. Great "mysteries" are great novels, and many great novels, like *Crime and Punishment, A Tale of Two Cities,* or *The Scarlet Pimpernel,* are clearly mysteries.

Bruce Cassiday, former fiction editor of *Argosy* magazine, has written radio and television scripts, magazine stories and novelettes, and over 60 novels and nonfiction books. From this background he gives us a careful and penetrating analysis of the various categories in the mystery field.

Note how he emphasizes the merry-go-round of the book and short story world. For this reason there is no listing of markets and no advice on where to send your manuscripts. *Writer's Digest* performs this function and can be picked up on nearby newsstands.

2. Into Something Rich and Strange

by Bruce Cassiday

The dizzying speed with which the fictional fad of one decade suffers a sea change into something rich and strange to become the prevailing genre of the next decade should be an inspiration at once stimulating and terrifying for any writer.

No matter what the manifestation of the mystery novel, the form has a fantastic survival rate in a field where other genres are pulped in the thousands by recycling machines for cereal cardboard each year.

This mysterious durability calls for analysis, but reducing art to its components and classifying it in categorical terms can be a deadly game.

Few writers — even geniuses — have written exclusively out of artistic inspiration. Every intuitive creator must at times sit back and consider the situs of art, simply to take stock of where he has been and where he is going.

It is in this spirit that analysis of recent trends in mystery fiction is undertaken — not to reduce the creation to molecules and atoms, but to observe the whole in its relation to past and future; inevitably, to see the present in terms of eternity.

This study will not show the writer how to follow the market, but how to recognize the various wellsprings of the literary fountainhead and put them to his own uses.

The analysis relies on mystery novels rather than on short stories, even though great ones appear even today, when the short story market is a failing shadow of its former self. A combination of fiscal evils — inflation, rising costs, postal rates, labor — has applied the blunt instrument to the magazine business, so that most of the mystery short story writers of a decade ago are now regularly producing novels. Examination of the magazines still extant will show trends similar to those exhibited in the novels mentioned here.

I am indebted to the late beloved Anthony Boucher, mystery critic for the New York *Sunday Times Book Review,* for a list of mystery genres he discussed in the original edition of this handbook published in 1956. He divided mystery novels into these five categories: the puzzle, the whodunit, the hard-boiled, the pursuit, and the straight novel. A comparison of the types of novels then in vogue with those of a comparable period some 20 years after should disclose interesting directions and divisions that can be used as signposts to anyone studying the mystery for pleasure or profit.

The "puzzle" mystery. The classic, simon-pure detective story, in which the author poses a problem and sets up a fair-play game of wits between detective and reader. (Characteristic authors: Ellery Queen, John Dickson Carr, Agatha Christie.)

After 20-odd years, the "puzzle" novel, as Boucher described it, remains virtually the same — an old form, aging, but very nicely handled by its practitioners. (Agatha Christie, Andrew Garve, Michael Gilbert.)

The hard-boiled mystery. Occasionally a puzzle, usually a whodunit, but primarily an adventure story of the violent physical exploits of a vigorous super-hero, generally a private detective. (Raymond Chandler, Brett Halliday, Ross Macdonald, Mickey Spillane. Boucher noted that he had purposely left out Dashiell Hammett, who stood alone in his craft. Amen.)

More than two decades have treated the "hard-boiled" novel rather unkindly. The tough, disillusioned hero found just as much to be disillusioned about after World War II as he did in the 30s. It now features a detective, insurance investigator, skip-tracer or whatever as protagonist, and tends to use harsher, tougher prose than the ordinary private-eye novel. (Ross Macdonald, John D. MacDonald, Joe Gores, Michael Collins, Ross Thomas.)

The straight mystery. A perfectly straight novel of character analysis and character interplay that happens to concern a crime, usually murder. (Frances Iles, Elisabeth Sanxay Holding, Matthew Head.)

The straight novel marketed as a mystery is still a true literary form after more than 20 years, blending the familiar characteristics that make it a mystery with good novelistic professionalism. (Nicolas Freeling, Julian Symons, Harry Kemelman, Georges Simenon.)

Conversely, many mysteries are marketed as straight novels in order to get better market penetration among those readers who deny the category. Regard the following best-selling crypto-crime novels of recent years:

The Blue Knight, Joseph Wambaugh; *Report to the Commissioner,* James Mills; *The Andromeda Strain,* Michael Crichton; *The Godfather,* Mario Puzo; *The Exorcist,* William Peter Blatty; *Day of the Jackal,* Frederick Forsyth; *Tinker, Tailor, Soldier, Spy,* John Le Carré; *Harlequin,* Morris West; *The Moneychangers,* Arthur Hailey.

The idea seems to be that if you want to be a best-selling mystery novelist — and who doesn't? — write a mystery novel that isn't one.

Incidentally, the non-existent category continues to thrive!

The novel of pursuit. Usually a story of espionage but sometimes of private excitement in which the question is not *Why?* or *How?* but *What will happen next?* or *How can he get out of this?* (Eric Ambler, Geoffrey Household, Dorothy B. Hughes, Cornell Woolrich.)

The upsurge of the novel of pursuit and action in its four-odd current guises is an interesting counter-trend to the direction noted by Anthony Boucher in 1956 when he said that the novel of pursuit had almost disappeared in the first decade after the Second World War.

Today this form is strongly back in the running in four basic guises, producing a large number of espionage, geopolitical, and even metaphysical novels.

The novel of pursuit generally stresses extroversion over introversion. Even when it deals with demonic possession and madness, the emphasis is on the outer trappings of action and terror rather than on psychological analysis.

And, when it deals with technology and the mechanics of today's world, the stress is definitely on the *way things are done* rather than on the people who are doing them; on the make and model of the gun or weapon used for the killing or maiming rather than on the perpetrator using the weapon; on the method of pursuit, entrapment, or capture rather than on the personalities of the hunter and the hunted.

This concentration on methodology and technology is perhaps the most revolutionary change in mystery prose during the period. There is no question that the mechanistic, technological mystery is holding up a true mirror to the dehumanized, impersonal, thing-dominated culture of today.

The pursuit sub-types are the "spy," "man-on-the-run," "metaphysical," and "doomsday" novels.

The spy mystery. The efforts of a professional agent to cope with his opposite number and sometimes his own superiors, in a taut, cold-war situation. (John Le Carré, Len Deighton, Ian Fleming.)

The man-on-the-run mystery. The reactions of a man suddenly thrust into an international situation, with or without social and/or political overtones, in which the suspense is based on the question *What is happening, and how the hell do I get out of it?* (Frederick Forsyth, Eric Ambler, Geoffrey Household, Alistair Maclean.)

The metaphysical mystery. An offspring of the classic gothic of "Monk" Lewis and the Mesdames Shelley and Radcliffe, dealing with the possession of souls, Black Masses, ghosts, and the occult, with the pursuit modeled on the Greek drama — man hectored by demons or by gods. (Tom Tryon, William Peter Blatty, Ira Levin.)

[NOTE: The 'metaphysical" mystery, although an offspring of the classic gothic, bears little resemblance to the "modern gothic," the romantic mystery novel discussed with skill, affection, and knowledgeability by Phyllis Whitney, one of its most noted practitioners, in other pages of this handbook.]

The doomsday mystery. A geopolitical study of the way a protagonist copes with such world-destroyers as atom bombs, nerve gas, and mutant microbes. (Tom Ardies, Robert Traver, John Lange.)

The whodunit. A story whose plot is still the solution of a crime, with a surprise ending (in intent, at least) and usually with a detective, but with little stress on deductions or challenging the reader's wits and primary emphasis on the emotions and reactions of the characters. (Mary Roberts Rinehart, Craig Rice, Mignon G. Eberhart.)

The whodunit had begun to break out of its strictures of style and content even by 1956, and Boucher included the "informal whodunit" as a sub-type. It is a fusion of the strict whodunit and the straight novel, with overtones of psychological, sociological, and political problems replacing romance as the chief interest. (William Campbell Gault, Ben Benson, Lawrence Treat.)

During the intervening years the whodunit has continued to proliferate at an amazing rate. Out of the basic form, new and important sub-types have emerged which use the apparatus of the whodunit but shift the emphasis from crime solution to other interests.

Among the more obvious sub-types are: the sociopolitical, police procedural, psychological, mechanistic, vigilante, caper, camp, and period mysteries.

By far the most significant development in mystery publishing in the recent years is the growth of the mystery novel devoted to societal issues — the "socio-political" mystery novel. Its purpose is to explore global problems, race, the underprivileged, and the plight of man in an upside-down world.

It is to the credit of the extremely adaptable whodunit form that the "socio-political" mystery accounts for the largest single sub-type today. The next largest sub-type is the "police procedural" mystery, a slightly altered form of the old detective and country-house whodunit.

Here are the nine sub-types of the durable old whodunit, defined with their most important practitioners:

The socio-political mystery. The protagonist tries to survive the explosion of social unrest, technological disaster, or political confrontation that are part of all our lives today. (Dorothy Salisbury Davis, Jack Higgins, Chester Himes, Peter Driscoll.)

The police procedural mystery. A story of a real police detective working on a real police force, solving one crime or a series of crimes, the events narrated in an almost documentary fashion. (Ed McBain, Lawrence Treat, Hillary Waugh, John Creasey, Lesley Egan, Robert L. Pike (Fish), Richard Martin Stern.)

The private-eye mystery. A story of crime-solution in which the detective may be an investigator of any kind — insurance, skip-tracer, lawyer, or ordinary citizen in the role of investigator. (Rex Stout, John D. MacDonald, Aaron Marc Stein, Harold Q. Masur, Herbert Brean, Richard Lockridge, Dick Francis, George Harmon Coxe, Judson Philips.)

The psychological mystery. A story of inner malaise affecting the lives of people personally related to the protagonist, usually involving the solution of a murder. (Stanley Ellin, Margaret Millar, John Farris.)

The mechanistic mystery. A novel stressing the mechanics and techniques of a larger-than-life endeavor in the business and/or political world, with method and technology over-shadowing the people. This is the macrocosm of the same world the socio-political mystery views in microcosm. (Paul E. Erdman, Federick Forsythe, Michael Crichton.)

The vigilante mystery. A whodunit in which the "who" is discovered early on, so that stress can be laid on the chase, capture, and subsequent punishment of the guilty, sometimes with sado-masochistic overtones, and generally with socio-political intent. (Joe Gores, Brian Garfield, Bill Pronzini.)

The caper mystery (the yin-yang opposite of the straight whodunit). A step-by-step analysis of a crime as it is planned by the man who is going to bring it off. (Eric Ambler with *Topkapi,* Richard Stark, Lionel White.)

The camp mystery. The rules and appurtenances of any of the foregoing sub-types turned inside out and played strictly for belly laughs. (Donald E. Westlake, Ed McBain, Robert L. Fish.)

The period mystery. A novel of mystery in any of the foregoing sub-types set in the past, usually dealing with crime or murder and stressing the social and political values of the other time. (John Dickson Carr, Robert van Gulick, Nicholas Meyer with *The Seven Percent Solution.*) Cinema's *Chinatown* and *The Sting* were original, period mysteries written for film rather than for print.

If any one thing is apparent from this review of several decades of mystery publishing, it is that the Second World War divided mystery literature into the quick and the dead just as surely as it divided the safe and wonderful world of yesterday from today's frightening and unstable technological world.

Like it or not, the Second World War changed the mystery story from a tale of death to a tale of megadeath, from a tale of deductive simplicity to a tale of scientific complexity, and from a tale of simple treasure or stolen loot to a tale of missing atomic formulas or lost psyches.

Likewise, it shifted the mystery story from the drawing rooms of the solid middle (or upper) class to the streets and alleys of a troubled populace in social, racial, political, and economic ferment.

At the same time, and far more significantly, it shifted the emphasis of the genre from the individual to the group. Sherlock Holmes operated as a one-man puzzle-solving entity. So did Sam Spade, Philip Marlowe and Lew Archer. But note what has happened in the past two decades: The police procedural novel has come of age and already begun to wither. So has the spy novel. Both deal with groups rather than individuals. So do the socio-political mystery, the caper, vigilante, doomsday, and mechanistic mysteries.

Policeman, spy, scientist, heister, vigilante — each is one of a group. So is the man saving the world from fire, flood, or plague. And so is the master mind of an enormous monetary or political coup.

As our own lives have been forced to shift their emphasis from the individual to the group, so has our fiction: a trend well noted and examined by our art.

Masters of the art of fiction have always been influenced by the trends and directions of the time. Scott influenced Balzac; Balzac influenced Dickens; Dickens influenced Hardy. Yet each is distinct and individual. Each produced art by using basic themes and imbuing them with his own attitude and style.

It is up to the writer of each age to see the patterns and purposes of its mores and the directions of its art — and then throw away all the charts and graphs and invent a new image for the age to be remembered by.

More than any other type of novel except the novel of manners, of which it is a viable sub-type, the mystery novel holds up the mirror to society in our troubled age. Though the scene in that mirror be unpleasant, those gazing at it must always be stirred in some way — to fear, regret, terror, humor, inspiration. To stir the reader is the writer's whole purpose. It is he who turns the mirror to the proper angle — for his own enlightenment, as well as the enlightenment of future generations. Remember that it is not crime, or the fact of evil that is important to the mystery writer, but the way we, as artists, view evil and what we do about it.

3. Where Do You Get Your Ideas?

The question most frequently asked of writers is where they get their ideas. It's a wide, wide field, as you'll see from the answers to the second question. Its exact phrasing is as follows: As far as you are concerned, what kind of idea furnishes you with the germ or seed of a story which ultimately flowers into the full story? That is, how does a story begin for you? An unusual character? Overheard dialogue? News clipping? Gimmick? A few details, please. And so — here are the details.

RICHARD MARTIN STERN reflects some 36 per cent of the answers when he says:

Damn near anything can trigger a story idea, as far as I can see — a snatch of a song, a remembered incident that didn't seem important at the time, a situation I read or hear about. Something catches my enthusiasm, and from then on I wonder, what if this and what if that? At last a story emerges.

JOHN CREASEY says the same thing:

Any incident — odd phrase — imagined situation. Seldom the same way twice in a row.

Few writers rely regularly on any one source, but 15 per cent of those who answered said they were usually sparked off either by a newspaper item or by some personal experience, 14 per cent worked from character, 10 per cent from background, and only 6 per cent from gimmick. But let them speak for themselves.

MIGNON G. EBERHART says that anything can start her off, and then adds:

Usually, I think, a writer is born with a sort of talent for observation; one is rather like a blotting paper; one soaks up everything almost without knowing it. As some friend of mine once said, however: "I know a little about a great many things."

ROSS MACDONALD says:

My plots nearly always begin with an idea for a basic reversal of what appears to be the case. Sometimes these ideas are drawn from life, and sometimes not.

JOHN D. MACDONALD is philosophical and concludes with a colorful example:

An idea useful in fiction of any length is the result of perceiving a relationship, an inner cry of "Aha!" The writer is a complexity of inputs, and of unselective recall. The sound of hail on the car roof ten years ago, and the glimpse, today, of a child pushing an empty wheelchair can trigger the perception of a relationship which can result in the soberest novel or the most gimmicky short story.

POUL ANDERSON has a similar comment:

Usually for a short story, and always for a novel, several different ideas must fuse. Sometimes a section, in itself too slight, will lie in the file for years — then suddenly another comes along, the old one catalyzes it, and a basic plot is there.

BRUCE GRAEME suggests an unusual way of starting:

Occasionally a good title gives me the theme of the story. It is my favorite way, especially as it saves me a day's thought, thinking of a title when I haven't one.

MARY BARRETT likes the method:

The best way for me to write a story is to begin with a title and see what develops. Frequently by the time the story is finished, the title no longer applies; but who cares?

EDWARD D. HOCH sometimes uses the title method:

A story usually begins with a gimmick or unusual situation, often suggested by a news report or something in a book. Often the title comes first and the story is built around it, though as the story develops, that original inspiring title might well be discarded.

DAN MARLOWE says tersely:

A gimmick, usually. Something to get it off to a fast start.

ROBERT L. FISH lines up on the same side:

Basically gimmick, especially for short stories. In novels, I like to establish an impossible situation and then show the situation is not only *not* impossible, but that any other situation would be abnormal. (The value of a dead snake; a man carrying a briefcase full of blocks of newsprint chained to his wrist, etc.)

ALAN K. YOUNG gives some interesting examples of a gimmick:

So far, almost all my published stories (most of which have revolved around codes or other plays on the language) have sprouted from what I suppose you would call gimmicks, *e.g.,* an English word that has changed meaning over the centuries, a Biblical verse that contains every letter of the alphabet but one, the tremendous odds against a paragraph occurring in English without any *e's,* the dying words of a famous person.

FRED TOBEY, a designer of automatic machinery as well as a short story writer, gives us a concrete example of the use of specialized knowledge gained in the practice of his profession. In the course of his explanation, he gives us an insight into how he builds a story. He tells us:

Every machinist knows that once in a while you find a brass nut that doesn't have any threads on it. Suppose someone murdered a man by loosening a nut on a machine so that the nut would fall off at a critical time. Suppose, after the accident, he had to put a new nut on quickly and got hold of a nut that didn't have any threads on it. Out of this came a story for me.

DOROTHY B. HUGHES tells us:

The germ or seed was always a place, a background scene. And against that background, there began a dialogue or monologue; whatever it was, it was conversation. Then I would begin to form the characters, or perhaps better to say, to recognize the characters. The plotting was the final step; it was people and place which interested me, not gimmicks.

MANNING LEE STOKES is a former newspaperman, and the profession left its mark on him:

Mostly I use newspaper clips. Occasionally an idea springs full blown from the head, but not often. Stories are everywhere if you can see them. This faculty can be learned, I suppose, or sharpened, but it is better to be born with it — the ability to "know a story." I do not think newspaper work helps a fiction writer all that much, but it does develop a story sense.

MIRIAM ALLEN DEFORD says simply:

Often a news clipping. Always a situation involving a problem. Then I visualize people in it and set them to working out the problem.

JANET GREGORY VERMANDEL says:

A news item may suggest a certain kind of business that seems to have possibilities, and then I work out a plot to fit. Often the original idea mutates during the writing process, or vanishes entirely, having acted as a catalyst in attracting other elements which eventually become the story.

DONALD OLSON will have nothing of the methods just cited:

Oddly enough, considering the richness of their material, news stories have rarely given me a useable idea; perhaps because they are not allusive enough. Seldom, either, does a gimmick *per se.* For me it's most often an unusual character or a scrap of overheard dialogue: a woman complaining in an airport about a tardy arrival, the haunting memory of a woman's ravaged features seen through the gloom of a tawdry movie theatre years ago, not infrequently a place like a country graveyard, deserted house, even an art museum.

A number of writers work from character, like WILLIAM P. McGIVERN:

An unusual character. I like to examine a character who believes he has full self-knowledge. In a crisis he learns otherwise, *e.g.,* the man who vows vengeance but learns he lacks vindictiveness, ruthlessness, or plain courage.

PHIL RICHARDS:

The best ideas come out of a dominant character trait, the classic example being the one about Alexander Woollcott, a house guest of Moss Hart, who complained that Woollcott got up in the middle of the night and rearranged the furniture. "You're lucky," someone commented, "that he's here only for the weekend. Suppose he broke a leg?" Hart looked at Kaufman, and *The Man Who Came To Dinner* was born.

I've sold many stories pivoting on odd facts: there's no *rigor mortis* in death from carbon-monoxide poisoning; carnations placed near a rock combo will soon lean away from it; British naval officers do not stand when they toast their sovereign; the Malay affliction of latah makes the victim a compulsive mimic.

HELEN WELLS:

A story starts for me with an emotional charge about *one* person. That person may be a man seen on the street with an expression on his face that makes me wonder: "What has happened to him?" Or I may overhear the person. Once in a restaurant booth, I overheard two middle-aged women saying of their mother: "Anne [their sister in law] locks her in her room and actually doesn't give her enough to eat!" What sort of son would permit that? So for me a story starts with a character.

RICHARD S. PRATHER's system involves an inordinate amount of work, which underlies his remarkable success:

During the course of my "plotting" (about 100,000 words of thinking-at-the-typewriter before beginning my first draft) several ideas develop, or take on an extra dimension, and the best of these generally become, together, the multiple-germ idea around which a "Shell Scott" book forms. Say there are five of those "best" ideas that intrigue me; the rest of my plotting is largely concerned with developing them further and joining each of them to all the others.

JOHN BALL also works constantly, although in a different and easier way:

Usually ideas come to me at any time and under any circumstances, simply because I am attuned to be receptive to them. It is my practice to keep pen and paper handy at *all* times, next to my bed at night, in my pocket during the day, even beside the swimming pool. When an idea does come I write it down immediately, because ten minutes later often won't do — they can come quickly and go just as rapidly, despite the certainty at the moment that they will be remembered. They won't be — so I write them down.

DANA LYON digs into her mind and gives an account of the origin of one of her books. She says:

Several years ago some members of my family had a kind of reunion in a cabin high in the mountains and completely off the beaten trail. One night, as my family sat around the fire, I told them the story of the *Mary Celeste,* found drifting and deserted in the middle of the ocean, with food still on the table. No one has ever solved the mystery. But looking around the cabin, I thought, supposing some people were up here having a good time, and then totally disappeared. It is dark, it is stormy, house is in perfect order, the car still stands outside, the half-eaten dinner is cold and congealed, and three people are gone. Why?

Most of us have wondered whether you can dream a story. Can you translate a dream onto paper, or does it wither away and seem never to have been?

LAURETTE P. MURDOCK touches on dreams as a source for stories when she writes:

For me, a story idea often comes from overheard dialogue, from clippings, or a fragment of a dream that persists, kicks around for a while and won't go away. A dream-envisioned title, "Uncle Pluto" — just that and nothing more — turned into a story published by *Audience.*

CHARLES M. PLOTZ, however, dreamt a whole story that was basically usable.

ERIC AMBLER concedes that he has to do far more than dream. He says:

For me, the full story only "flowers" through rewriting and often discarding the original stimulant.

PHYLLIS WHITNEY, ELINOR CHAMBERLAIN and MICHAEL BUTTERWORTH start with background.

WHITNEY:

I like to pick an interesting locality first, so that I can have a background in mind. This may be a place here or abroad that I visit on purpose to get material, or an area in my own locality — or even a place that is altogether imaginary. Once my background is set, I look for a heroine with a serious problem. As I put her down in the setting, one affects the other, and the story and characters begin to develop.

CHAMBERLAIN:

My stories begin with a geographical setting and a leading character who has recently arrived there. Other characters, indigenous to the scene, appear slowly and spontaneously. The plot grows from the people, the place, and the time.

BUTTERWORTH:

A story, for me, begins with the setting. All sorts of unlikely places contain an element of mystery and surprise. The Edwardian villas at the top of the beach in Trouville struck me very forcibly this summer: something will have to come out of my encounter with a place. The story line is almost the last consideration. The basic plot should turn on something extraordinarily simple; the trick is to make it seem otherwise.

CLAYTON MATTHEWS is one of those who start with an ending and work backwards:

In a short story, it is almost always the last line, or at least the last paragraph: this must be firmly fixed in my mind before I can write a story.

VIRGINIA B. MCDONNELL is sparked off by an outraged sense of justice:

My best stories come from things that bug me, things about which I feel strongly. Drugs, for example. Land grabs, vandalism, the proposed closing of our city's greenhouses. Starting from such a point, I can present a strong case for the changes *I* want. This doesn't mean I'm trying to write messages; rather, I'm trying to write about the things that seem to matter — with a dollop of humor.

THOMAS PATRICK MCMAHON's conscience works similarly:

For me, it has always started the same way — with the theme — not who did it, but what universal truth (if any) does the story illustrate.

GLORIA AMOURY has no illusions:

Afraid I do it coldbloodedly, commercially. I get my background first and then dream up a conflict endemic to that, provided it's a conflict for which I feel I have some empathy. The characters come later.

For PAULINE SMITH, research pays off:

The written word does it for me — like the local news item about a dog painted to death, which shocked me into a self-fulfilling prophecy story. The magazine article on quilting that led me to research quilt names and patterns, and sewed up a story on amateur detection through quilt blocks and their meanings. The book on guns in which I discovered the Colt action to be clockwise and the Smith & Wesson counterclockwise, which shot me right into a Russian roulette gimmick plot.

MAUREEN DALY is emotional:

For me a story usually begins with my happening on something poignant, frightening or intensely dramatic — it could be anything from a newspaper clipping to the disturbing sight of a neglected house, or someone very much alone on a busy street. Currently I am working on a novella which has its genesis in the tragic drowning of a six-year old boy in our farm pond about four years ago. I didn't see it, but I felt the terrible pain of the 12-year old brother who stood on the bank and saw his brother drown.

ROBERT LOUIS STEVENSON, a non-member who might well have joined MWA had he lived a hundred years later, started *Treasure Island* from an unusual springboard, and he gives us some sage advice. In his preface he says that it all began with a map that he drew one afternoon, for lack of anything better to do. Later, poring over his map, he saw characters and people in it, and he went on to write *Treasure Island.* He says:

It is perhaps not often that a map figures so largely in

a tale; yet it is always important. The author must know his countryside, whether real or imaginary, like his hand . . . .

It is my contention . . . that he who is faithful to his map, and consults it, and draws from it his inspiration, gains positive support, and not mere negative immunity from accident . . . . As he studies it (the map), relations will appear that he had not thought upon. He will discover obvious though unsuspected short-cuts and footpaths for his messengers; and even when a map is not all the plot, as it was in *Treasure Island,* it will be found to be a mine of suggestion.

Perhaps ROSS MACDONALD's remarks from "On Crime Writing" can best wind up this discussion. He says:

Detective novels differ from some other kinds of novels in having to have a rather hard structure built on logical coherence. But the structure will fail to satisfy the mind, writer's or reader's, unless the logic of imagination, tempered by feelings and rooted in the subconscious, is tied to it, often subverting it. The plans for a detective novel in the making are less like blueprints than like travel notes set down as you once revisited a city. The city has changed since you last saw it. It keeps changing around you. Some of the people you knew there have changed their names. Some of them wear disguises.

Now that the orchestra has given its overture, a few solo performances will elaborate the themes. The next four chapters are reprinted *in toto* from the earlier edition, reprinted because they are so clear and graphic that they could hardly be improved upon.

In this chapter, Fred Brown takes you by the hand and leads you on a guided tour through his mind -- or at least the highly developed professional part of it.

He had an unusual way of incubating and developing his plots. Once he had decided on his basic idea, he'd go to the nearest bus terminal and board the first transcontinental bus to leave. He'd travel for hours or days, with no concern as to where he went, while his book idea germinated. When it was ready, he'd phone his wife and tell her he was starting home.

This catalysis of motion is not unusual. When I lived near New York, I found that in the course of the hour's train ride to the city I often came up with a story idea or else the solution to some story problem. Bruno Fischer would get in a car and drive anywhere. Walking, riding, plane travel — motion of some sort frequently seems to set off the creative process.

4. Where Do You Get Your Plot?

by Fredric Brown

It is my belief — and I can be wrong; I have been — that all writers use identically the same system in plotting, but that very few have ever consciously analyzed the process. It's ridiculously simple. Now don't get me wrong; I don't mean that it's ridiculously simple to get a good plot, but I mean that the *process* by which a plot is created is easy to explain and easy to understand. And knowledge of the process as a conscious one enables one to retrace steps until the bug in a poor plot can be found and eliminated.

A writer plots by accretion. If you've forgotten what the word means I'll save you a trip to the dictionary — it means *increase by gradual addition.*

It can start with anything — a character, a theme, a setting, a single word. By accretion it builds or is built into a plot. I'll show you what I mean in a minute — demonstration is better than explanation any day of the week — but there are a few things I want to say first to get them out of the way.

The first dozen or thousand steps of the process may be subconscious. In most cases at least a few of the steps are subconscious and that's why writers who haven't analyzed the process fail to realize that certain steps have already taken place by the time they start consciously working on the plot in question. They are in the position of a woman who suddenly learns she is pregnant and doesn't know how it happened. Yes, I know, that woman would have to be pretty promiscuous in order not to know, but the simile still holds; the human mind is promiscuous in its thinking, never true to a single thought or even a single train of thought. And by the time it recognizes that it has a plot idea which is ready to be whipped into shape as a plot, it has forgotten where the plot idea came from.

That's why some writers are embarrassed at the stock question, "Where do you get your plots?" They really don't know how to answer; they explain, if they care to, how they whip a plot into shape, but they don't know where the plot came from. Therefore they can't give the true and simple answer: "Plots aren't 'got'; they are constructed one step at a time."

All right, now I'll demonstrate. Both hands empty and nothing up either sleeve. I'll start from complete scratch — a single word — and built it toward a plot. Not into a complete ready-to-start-writing-on plot, no, because to describe every single thought process that goes into the construction of a plot might take ten times as many words — or a hundred times as many — as will go into the actual story written from that plot. And actually I'm more interested in demonstrating a process than in "getting" a plot.

Of course I've got to decide first what kind of story I want to write. Since mystery novels are my main racket, I'll make it a plot for a mystery novel.

Now to pick a starting point — *any* starting point. Wait till I call to my wife who, at this moment, is enjoying herself out in the open air, mowing the lawn, while I slave over a hot typewriter. "Hey, Beth, give me a word! Any word!" (I could probably think of a word all by myself, but it might be one my subconscious has already been promiscuous with and then I'd be cheating you without knowing it.)

"Huh?" she calls back.

Well, that's a word and I *could* start from it, but she didn't really mean it as an answer to my question, so it doesn't count. And the lawnmower has stopped now so I'll explain. Intermission.

I went out and explained. She happened to be standing by the edge of the pool and looked down. The pool contains goldfish. Twenty-four goldfish in a pool seven feet across and a foot and a half deep. "Goldfish," she said. Naturally.

So now I'm back at the typewriter again. Tried, on my way back here, to keep my subconscious from doing any pushups on the word *goldfish,* and if it did I couldn't detect them.

Except for one thing, one important thing. I can't help realizing that my wife rolled a natural. I probably *will* write a mystery novel about goldfish. Don't know why I didn't think of it myself. Except that in the six months since those goldfish have owned me I've started only one new novel and had reason — irrelevant here — for making that a carnival background story. Until six months ago, when we bought a house in Venice, the only way I could tell goldfish from sardines was the fact that goldfish live in water and sardines live in olive oil. But I'm almost an expert on goldfish now, since so many of them came with the house. A few casualties among them — there were twenty-eight of them seven months ago when we bought the place — sent me to the library for books on goldfish and I've learned quite a bit about them. And by drawing on one or two of those books again I can throw in a lot of patter that will make me sound like an expert. Good background stuff always helps. So.

Goldfish. Murder in the Goldfish Pool. Corny, forget it.

Although there *has* been murder in my goldfish pool. Whenever one of the goldfish gets sick the others attack it and worry it to death pushing it around. Until I learned to isolate temporarily any fish the others started to heckle. But

I don't know enough of what a goldfish thinks about — although I've wondered — to write a story about goldfish only. I'd better get myself some human characters and human motives.

Protagonist maybe who has a collection of goldfish in a pool like mine? Could be, but I think a pet shop would give me a better setting, more people around, more doing. Pet shop specializing in goldfish and goldfish supplies. Somebody murdering goldfish? But why? Mmmm — that's going to be a toughie. Unless my murderer is a cat, and I'd better make him human or my publishers won't like it. But what could be the *effect* of murdering goldfish — what sane motive could there be? Well, financial loss to the owner of the goldfish, the owner of the pet shop. Somebody — my murderer, let's call him X — wants to buy the pet shop.

Why? Mmmm — let's get a picture of him first. He's got to have some kind of a criminal motive; let's make him an embezzler. (Where did that come from? Just read a chapter in a fact-crime book about "The Wily Wilby" — one of the cleverest embezzlers of all time.) As treasurer or chief bookkeeper or something of a big company he's been embezzling heavy dough. Model him after Wilby; that'll give me a good method of embezzling, if I have to describe it.

But how tie him in with the pet shop? He can be a customer there, but that isn't enough. An employee? That would be good, but how in hell . . .?

Got it. Embezzling isn't hard; an embezzler's trouble is that sooner or later his embezzlements will come to light no matter how clever he is, and the difficulty is in his making a safe getaway with the money before his embezzlements are found out — and in such a way that he'll never be caught after the law starts looking for him. So — this has been done before, but so has everything else — suppose X's plan consists in building himself a second identity right in the same town *before* he makes his break? Then the cops will be hunting him all over the country and he'll be right here in an identity already established and accepted as being someone else.

Part-time job, it would have to be. At least while he's building the other identity. Let's say the proprietor of the pet shop — I think he's going to be my protagonist, and I can work in love or sex interest with a female employee — advertises for a part-time employee to keep the shop open evenings (I can work out a reason for that) and the embezzler sees that as his chance and, in disguise, takes the job. Builds himself double life, lives two places — both with private entrances so he can change his disguise in either — embezzles by day, and by evening works in the pet shop. In his first identity makes himself an occasional customer of the pet shop by day as an advance check on whether his dual identity is foolproof — and also to let me get him into the story as a character *both* ways, but apparently as two separate characters. Probably each a little eccentric, but in different ways.

Let's see, we can open the story about the time the proprietor learns with surprise that a customer of his, let's call him Mr. Janney, has blown town with four hundred thousand hard-embezzled dollars. We'll have to establish him as a customer in retrospect; that's all right, though. But before we establish him at all, we've got to establish Willis Dean, the rather eccentric character with red hair who is now working for Henry Burke (might as well give our pet shop proprietor a name) for several months now, establish him so firmly with the reader that the reader won't suspect the truth.

Want a narrative hook to start with — something to get things going before the detective drops in (by day) to ask questions about Mr. Janney, since the detective had learned Janney had bought a few goldfish from Burke. Shenanigans with goldfish, of course. Burke's goldfish are starting to die off mysteriously. (And in some way that would make it seem that his night man, Willis, couldn't have done it. Keep the reader from suspecting Willis of anything; better make him a very likable eccentric, that will help.)

But now we're back to where we started; *why* would any-one murder goldfish? Only now we can answer it because we've built some characters and a situation. The embezzler, in his new and unsuspected character as Willis Dean, has a long range and carefully worked out plan to let himself get to the stage where he can enjoy the fruits of his embezzle-ment. (What good would four hundred thousand dollars do him if he's got to keep on living on the scale of being a part-time employee of a pet shop?) He's already carefully planted the fact that he's got some — not too much — savings. He wants our protagonist to start losing money so he can buy in as a partner first and then, after more losses, buy out his interest in it. And then . . . .

That's enough to show the method. It's a hell of a long way from a complete plot, of course; it's just a starting point. But it's something to work from, something to get my teeth into when I get around to figuring how I'm going to work in a murder or two — human beings, not goldfish. The crimi-nal automatically has a motive, though, for killing anyone who happens to find out the truth, so there's no difficulty there. That disguise business is going to take a lot of thought to make it sound, and be, credible. But I think it can be worked out without seeming artificial or incredible.

But whether or not that particular start of a plot can ever be worked into a good sound plot, it's enough to show how plots are worked out. Anyway, how mine are. There isn't a damn thing mysterious about it, and it works.

In the previous chapter Fred Brown talked about books, but his method is equally valid in constructing a short story. In this chapter Pauline Bloom, who has taught writing at Brooklyn College and has a writing course of her own, analyzes a story in depth. In my early writing days she held a sword over my head as she kept asking me, "What's the conflict?" And too many times the sword swung, and chopped my head off.

Listen to her, for her advice is valuable, and after you've read this chapter, analyze a story on your own. Pick a story that you like, of a type you'd like to write, and read it over three or four times. Then take it apart and examine its structure.

5. How to Achieve Story Structure

by Pauline Bloom

Most professional mystery writers agree that the best way to achieve good story structure is to work on that first. Of course this doesn't mean that other story factors must be abandoned, even in the preliminary stages. But don't get lost in the mood or emotional aspects of the story before you know how you want to use them, or they will mislead you.

Poe was a master of story structure. Here is his advice to the writer: "Nothing is more clear than that every plot worth the name must be elaborated to its denouement before anything be attempted with the pen. It is only with the denouement constantly in view that we can give a plot its indispensable air of consequence or causation, by making the incidents, and especially the tone at all points tend to the development of the intention."

Take away the verbosity of Poe's time, and what do we have? Plan your story before you write it. Know the end before you plot the middle.

Many of the writers with whom I work understand the importance of plot and conflict development, particularly in the mystery story. Their competence in other writing departments sometimes makes one wonder why they seem to find it so difficult to put this well-known principle of conflict development into practice in their own stories. They're quick enough to criticize this weakness in other writers. But there is an emotional resistance to the translation of this idea into action in their own stories. There are reasons for this, and you must understand them in order to be able to cope with the problem.

In the first place there is in all of us a natural resistance to hard work. Plotting the story is the hardest of hard work because it involves concentrated thinking instead of riding along with your emotions. We therefore develop a tendency to become preoccupied with busy work, like dreaming about a character's antecedents and how he once told off his boss — or like polishing a phrase here and a wonderful line of dialogue there.

Certainly I'm not minimizing the importance of characterization or dialogue or writing style. But you'll have a stronger, better integrated, more balanced story, and a better written one, too, if you leave the revisions for later. Plan your story carefully before you write it, so that you know where you're going and are sure there is enough conflict development on the way.

Another reason for insufficient or weak conflict development is this: in our personal lives, if we are at all well adjusted human beings, we have learned through the years to face each problem as it comes up, and to solve it in the most practical and expeditious way possible. Get it out of the way and on to the next problem. In writing fiction, the technique is just the reverse, and therefore unnatural from the standpoint of the personal emotions of the writer. You take a character you have created, with whom you therefore identify yourself immediately. He is in trouble. What is your first instinct? To get him out of trouble as fast as you know how. So what do you do? You get him out of trouble as fast as you know how.

But what does good story structure demand? Good story structure demands that you not only involve your main char-

acter in trouble, but that you resist the temptation to have
him work out his solution too promptly and too easily. In
good fiction, and in good mystery fiction particularly, the conflict must *grow*. The problem must become more and more
intense, before you allow him to solve it.

Save your kindly instincts for the real people around you.
In dealing with fictional characters, don't spare them at the
expense of story structure. Challenge them with strong conflicts that are worthy of them, and test them further by having
their first few efforts to extricate themselves not only fail,
but involve them even further with their difficulties. Let me
illustrate this point by examining an outstanding story, "The
Betrayers," by Stanley Ellin. Here is a synopsis of it. The
numerals will be explained later.

Through the thin wall that separates Robert from his
neighbor, he can hear a good deal of what goes on in her
room, and he falls in love with her. Gradually he learns more
and more about her.

(1) She is married. (2) Her husband, Vincent, is a bully
who abuses her. (3) The husband is violent — dangerous.
(4) He is apparently involved in a serious crime. (5) Amy
discovers it and reproaches him for it. (6) During the quarrel
which ensues, there are two hard blows and apparently a
body falls.

(7) Before Robert can pull himself together sufficiently
to face the murderer, there is the sound of a body being
pulled out of the room and down the stairs. Such a brazen
killer would certainly destroy anyone who faced him now.
Robert doesn't. (8) After the downstairs door clicks open and
shut again, Robert goes out into the hall, and halfway down
the stairs picks up a handkerchief with blood on it. (9) By
the time he gets back to his room, a car has roared away,
the murderer and the victim in it. (10) Call the police? There
is no evidence except the handkerchief, which can be ascribed
to a nosebleed. The police would laugh at him.

(11) As he is a professional credit researcher and knows the techniques of his trade, Robert decides to go back into the girl's life, and through her to search through Vince's past for something which would convince the police his story was worth looking into. He opens a letter addressed to Amy from her sister in a small upstate town, takes a few days off from his job, and begins to learn about Amy. Sister tells him father had thrown her out of the house because of some trouble with a man, or what the father chose to interpret as trouble.

(12) Sister then refers him to Amy's teacher, who tells him the school principal had tried to assault Amy and, when she cried out, had charged her with blackmailing him. Principal had then bullied both Amy and teacher into silence. (13) Amy had tried suicide.

(14) Teacher sends him to office where Amy got a job. Robert learns that the theft of some petty cash had been attributed to her because she was the prettiest and most "secretive," and so she'd been fired. When they discovered it was someone else, Amy was gone.

(15) Robert talks to girl who had been friendly with Amy and learns about Vince. He gets a snapshot of the foursome taken on a double date, searches newspaper records and learns of an unsolved bank holdup. He gets a bank manager to identify the thief from the snapshot and sign a statement. Every man who had come into Amy's life had in one way or another betrayed her, Robert realizes bitterly. At least he must help catch her last and worst betrayer.

(16) Police are cool to Robert's story until he produces the bank manager's statement. He accompanies police to his neighbor's room and, when they force their way in, there instead of Vince, stands Amy, "the same look on her face ... that she must have worn each time she came face to face with a betrayer." In trying to track down her supposed murderer, he had himself betrayed her more than any of her previous betrayers.

(17) Amy throws herself from the window and is killed.

Each numeral here indicates a step forward in the conflict development of this story. Basically, this is a love story which fate seems to have determined to thwart. From this point of view, everything that stands between Robert and Amy, such as her marriage, and every betrayal of Amy that Robert turns up is a conflict peak which brings Amy closer to her ultimate betrayal by Robert; and every step he takes in trying to track down Vincent is also a step which brings him closer to the final ironic climax of the story where he, the man who loves her, actually destroys her.

Now, how do you go about plotting a story of your own? There must be a strong, well-developed conflict. There must be growing tension and excitement. How are you going to achieve it?

The answer is: step by step. The prospect of working out a well-developed mystery plot is a formidable one, and if you face it all at once, you are apt either to put it off or else to come up with a story which really does not use your best potential. But if you take it one step at a time, and put everything else out of your mind except the one step on which you are working, the results are likely to be better.

You already have an idea as a jumping-off place. Whatever it is, pull it right into the conflict development area by asking yourself, "How will this idea give me a character facing a serious conflict or problem?" If it does, fine. Stay with it. If it doesn't, let it go — for the present.

Don't worry about not having story ideas. You can start working on a story, "without an idea in the world," (which, of course, on the face of it is impossible). Ask yourself the following questions and answer them. Go on, try it, and see what happens!

1. What kind of mystery story would it be a good idea for me to work on? On the basis of your experience, field of knowledge, personal leaning, or for any other reason you

wish, choose a mystery story type.

2. For this particular kind of story, what sort of person would be a good bet for a main character?

3. For such a character in such a story, what would be a good conflict or problem for him to face? What is he up against? What is he trying to achieve? What does he want so much at this particular period of his life that he's willing to fight to the end for it?

4. What are the obstacles to his achieving this goal? Whom or what does he have to overcome?

The first three questions are easy. Beginning with the fourth, they become more challenging, so let's accompany them with illustrations from "The Betrayers," previously synopsized.

In this story, Robert's objective is to help the girl he loves. He hasn't the courage to do anything for her before her supposed death, but after it he can at least track down her supposed murderer. The difficulty in his path is his lack of knowledge about her, her husband, or their past lives.

But on the emotional level, each time he takes a step which he believes brings him closer to trapping Vince, it actually brings him closer to trapping and betraying and bringing about the death of Amy herself. Therefore, the climax of the story reverses the significance of each conflict peak.

5. Put down in one sentence your main character's objective and difficulties. This will be your story nucleus. The story nucleus here might be something like this: Robert sets out to trap Vince, but his trail leads him and the police to Amy, so that he is himself the instrument of her death.

6. This is the most difficult step of all. Your story nucleus gives you the beginning and the end of your story. What you must do now is work out the middle, the part most frequently skimped or overlooked by inexperienced writers. Think through the middle of your story in such a way that the story line arranges itself in a series of peaks and valleys.

In "The Betrayers" there are, by my analysis, seventeen such conflict peaks, some more important than others. You don't need to have as many as this, but you must have enough to make your story interesting and suspenseful.

At this point it would be a good idea for you to read or reread a few of the more successful published mysteries, and analyze them yourself for conflict development, as I have done here with "The Betrayers." Then check your own conflict development against that of the published stories you've analyzed. If it seems to stand up, write a synopsis of all the story action.

Of course you still have the planning of the other story elements, and the actual writing and rewriting. But try tackling one problem at a time, and solving it before you go on to the next. Doing so will give you a feeling of security about the work behind you and will help you do the best writing you are capable of.

Hillary Waugh wrote this article at the beginning of his career. Thirty or more books later, his procedure is basically unchanged. If the proof of the pudding is in the eating, the proof of the working method is in the selling. And Hillary Waugh has not only sold, but in the course of the years he has developed to a stature that makes him one of the leading novelists of the genre.

As you read further on, you will find that other writers use other methods.

Which one should you use? The one that suits you best. And, although that sounds like an easy answer, it isn't. In the long run only experience, only trial and error can teach you where you belong.

6. Why I Don't Outline

by Hillary Waugh

Once I have the idea for the kind of book I want to write, I decide first who is to be murdered, then who kills him and for what reason. In working this much out I have to develop some background on both killer and victim, know something of their character and past life. With that in mind, I can now go on to the problem of how the killer is going to commit the crime, where and when.

At this point, if I have a gimmick, I know what the key is by which the detective will finally unlock the case, and if it involves the scene of the crime it is included. If there is no gimmick, this is the time to determine how the murder will eventually be solved. Some ideas can be gained through the knowledge of the crime I now have. If that isn't enough I will introduce variations, but at any rate this is where the general plot is thought out. To some extent the plot will be determined by the crime I've planned, but on the other hand the plot idea will alter the murder. Each works on the other, but the whole story develops at this point. In other words, I generally start with the scene of the murder and build from there.

Next comes the detective. The kind of detective he is, private eye or member of the regular force, is part of the original idea, but so far that's about all I know of him. His position will, of course, have an effect upon the plotting I've done since a private detective would work under a different set of rules from a police detective, but now his character has to be developed. To have the plot progress according to plan, the clues will have to be uncovered in a certain order. That will necessitate certain circumstances arising to make that happen, but it will also mean a careful planning of the character of the hero. Different people work in different ways and I'll need a particular type of person to move the way I want him to. Since this one person will have a strong impact on the story, he must be chosen with a view to having the effect desired.

Once the murderer, victim, evidence and detective have been established, the next step is plot complication. That means the introduction of other suspects with motives and clues that will involve them.

Lastly, since none of the characters will remain static during proceedings, I must now determine how each person will react to the pressures around him and how that can further cast or remove suspicion. Their behavior further complicates the plot, shifting the progress of the story one way or another, and the whole thing must be juggled into position so that the proper end develops.

As is apparent, the whole story until this point has been in a state of flux and outlining would have been completely useless. Everything is in my mind only.

I could now make out an outline if I chose. I don't for two reasons. One is that with the whole story committed to memory there is no need of an outline, and the other is that in the actual writing I find the story is still fluid. Though I know about what will take place, I don't know how the characters will behave. It has been my experience that characters tend to act independently from my will and the tight rein of an outline would warp them out of shape. The only way I can keep their behavior natural is to give them as much leeway as possible within the main framework of the story.

This is not to disparage outlining. A good many authors do outline and most successfully. In fact, those who *can* outline have a decided advantage in many ways. With the whole story in front of them, they can write faster and with less need for rewriting. In my own case, and this is a disadvantage, I have to write each story twice, and the first draft could be considered as a super-detailed outline for the second. In the final analysis, whether one outlines or doesn't is purely a matter of individual taste and no one can say that one method produces a better result than the other.

Being told what not to do is sometimes more valuable than being told what you should do, but unfortunately few writers like to admit their early mistakes. Dana Lyon, however, is an exceptional person, and in her own breezy, charming, frank and informal way, she relates some of her early troubles and turmoils in the course of turning out books that all of us would love to have written.

7. Plotting From a Situation

by Dana Lyon

For my money, there are three different ways of starting a book: you get a plot, you get some characters, or you get a situation. And go on from there.

My own personal method of writing is the last mentioned —the situation. Let's analyze the type of story that develops from a situation. One of my early books, *It's My Own Funeral,* was definitely a situation story which was one of the most difficult I ever wrote because I had not yet developed enough skill and craftsmanship to think it out before I wrote it. I was too entranced by the "situation"—a man regaining consciousness in a coffin on the way to his own funeral—to do more than marvel at my originality. That was the situation. All of it. Just a little innocent idea that popped into my head one day when there was nothing else in it. It seemed like such an elegant idea that I immediately sat down and started furiously writing the book—even the title was a natural. The only thing was, as I progressed more and more slowly, who was the man? Why was he in the coffin? How does he get out? Believe me, never again. Never again, I swore, would I sit down to write a book without having the last chapter clear in my mind.

If I may digress a moment, I think that is one of the most important elements for any mystery writer to possess—the knowledge of *where he is going*! It's like this: suppose you are making a trip from New York to San Francisco and have to be there within a certain time. You can make all the side trips you like; you can decide either to go by way of Chicago or by way of New Orleans, as long as eventually one or the other itinerary is decided upon. You can stop off at the Grand Canyon, you can dawdle through New Mexico, you can take a whack at Las Vegas; but you know that at the end you are going to turn up in San Francisco at a certain time. Thus with the mystery. You know where you are going, so you can take as many side trips as you want. But if you know only that you are leaving New York but not where you are heading, you are as likely as not to end up in Minnesota or Kansas, broke, hungry and jobless.

Because I didn't know where I was going, *It's My Own Funeral* was a stinker to write—and it was only by the grace of God and Rinehart that it ever got published. The crook turned out to be the cop, the private eye turned out to be the crook, the amateur detective couldn't solve the mystery (naturally, since *I* couldn't) and the heroine was homely. Or perhaps it was just that I was rebelling against every cliché in the field and wanted to blast them all. I did. As a postscript, I might add that the book sold *in spite* of the method I used, not because of it. I wouldn't advise anyone to follow my example.

The next "situation" book I wrote (that sold, I mean—let's skip the rest of them) was *The Frightened Child.* This was an idea I had been tinkering with for a number of years, had started half a dozen times, and finally managed to complete for the simple reason that at last I knew I was going from New York to San Francisco. The "situation" was this: a man and his wife each decide to murder the other, but the one who succeeds gets caught in his own trap. Do you see what I mean by a situation? Not characters, not plot, not a bare idea, but a story in one sentence, just as you'd say to an architect, "I want a Colonial house" or "I want a ranch-type house." The form is presented; but then the blueprints must be drawn up (oh, those horrible hours and days and weeks of just plain *thinking*). But after that the actual construction goes sailing along with only an occasional hitch here and there.

8. When and How Do You Write?

By now, you know something about how to construct a plot. You've studied theory, and you've looked over the shoulders of a few pros. You've been doing a considerable amount of thinking and you have a few ideas that are germinating in your mind, but before they push through to the surface and pop out, there are a few practical decisions to make. One of them concerns how you're going to organize yourself as a writer.

Perhaps you're wondering who follows which of the methods you've just read about, and you'd certainly like to hear a few details. There are plenty of details, and the questionnaire brought out much more than the stock answers you might have expected.

The question asked was: When and how do you write? Give us an outline of your working methods, please. Hours per day? A.M. or P.M.? Regularly or spasmodically? Copious notes or none at all?

There is a wide variety of methods of writing, but of the full-time writers all except a half-dozen or so had definite schedules. Some were morning workers, others afternoon or night workers. Some worked seven days a week, fifty-two weeks a year. Some were productive only during certain periods, but all stressed the importance of a working regimen.

JOHN D. MACDONALD sums it up:

One works whatever *regular* hours suit his own body chemistry and energy cycle. Any writer who writes only when he "feels like it" is perhaps not only an unsuccessful writer, but quite possibly an unsuccessful human being. (I am not using success in any strictly monetary sense.)

POUL ANDERSON, a careful and conscientious worker, integrates the methods and agonies of creation. He defines his process:

Much thinking, study, research, etc. beforehand; rather spasmodic and daydreamy at first, then more and more systematic as the ideas and story take shape. Notes on everything, maps, house plans, biographies of all characters of any importance, and so on. Finally, a typewritten first draft, during the doing of which I work long hours, neglect everything else, and get very unpleasant if interrupted. Each day's output is gone over several times with pencil, and likewise for the entire ms, until no one but I can read it. After the longest possible cooling-off period, I go through the thing again a couple of times, then type a second draft at a pretty high speed, though making numerous changes in the course of it as they occur to me. Again, the ms is set aside for as long as deadlines permit, then gone through just a couple of times, since by now only minor corrections seem in order — made on the script in ink.

Even so, on seeing the thing in print, I can still flinch and mutter, "Oh, no! How did that ever get by me?"

Almost every writer stressed the importance of preparation. Some, like CLAYTON MATTHEWS, put very little down on paper. He says:

> I believe that most writers are actually working during all waking hours. This certainly is the case with me, since the material is written in my mind before I ever approach a typewriter.

On the other hand, DAN MARLOWE works "from a detailed (5,000 words or more) outline."

ROSS MACDONALD writes:

> Three or four hours a day, five days a week, beginning late morning or noon, regularly. I make a great many notes, sometimes over a period of years, in one case 12 or 13 years. When things are going well, I write a thousand words a day and don't rewrite extensively, though of course I often have.

ERIC AMBLER works steadily and conscientiously:

> Five hours per day, every day, Sundays and holidays included, beginning immediately after an early breakfast. Back-of-envelope notes only.

Preparation is a 24-hour affair for DANA LYON:

> My writing is always done in the morning when my energies are fresh. My books start with an idea which I allow to germinate for awhile, then comes the period of intensive thinking before I put words to paper. I never make what could be called an outline (I am afraid that if I write the story down, it'll be out of me for good), just two or three pages of notes as ideas come to me. I keep separate pages for each character and write down their various aspects as I think of them, though I seldom glance at the pages again; they are already impressed on my mind. But like most writers, I think constantly, 24 hours a day, about the germinating book, and

when it's time to start writing it, I always know.

The late MARGARET MANNERS stressed both the constant, subconscious thinking and the training of that subconscious:

I cannot count those hours in which my brain was working on problems when it was trying to do other things. Talking with a friend, one word might make things fall into place. Some solutions are delivered as by computer: think of a problem before falling asleep; wake up with the answer.

HELEN WELLS mentions the same device:

Before going to sleep at night, I hold the story I'm working on in my mind and order my unconscious to think about it. On waking, often a new idea has surfaced — and I keep pen and paper at bedside to write it down immediately. Ditto pen and paper in my handbag, for ideas or scraps of dialogue that occur during the day.

I start by writing a biography and character study for each character. Plot grows out of character and the character's relationships.

Having once attempted to write a novel without an outline, and having seen it wander all over and peter out aimlessly — I learned early to know where (and how) the story is heading. So I work out an outline: first in big blocks, then chapter-by-chapter. Notes for each chapter go into the numbered pockets of a big manila folder (accordion style).

There's one danger to this method, which Phyllis Whitney pointed out to me: you may put your freshest energy and enthusiasm into the outlining, rather than into the actual writing.

Silence and solitude are my restoratives. At the same time, some simple physical activity or chore which keeps the forefront of my mind busy, releases the unconscious levels, and a story floats up.

LUCY FREEMAN, who has written both fiction and non-fiction, makes an interesting comment concerning the different working methods that the two forms involve. She says:

Each time (I write fiction) I postpone and postpone beginning the book. It is as though I must toss it around in my unconscious for weeks, even months, before I start. But once I do, the writing goes far more easily than in nonfiction, which, for me, means the slow work of organizing, of writing at least two or three drafts, of continually adding new facts, new thoughts. It seems that the painful part of fiction is getting started, while the painful part of nonfiction, whose research I can always plunge into without delay, comes in the actual work on paper.

CURTIS B. NORRIS speaks of the need to get ideas down on paper as soon as they occur:

A good lead can come to mind any time, and it usually picks the most inconvenient time to pop up — such as a five p.m. traffic jam. Then I'll run it over and over in my mind (for it is a fleeting, fragile, wispy thing) so I won't forget it before I can pull over and write it down. I often go to bed at night with my mind "programmed" onto a difficult plot turn, or a problem on how to weave true facts together in a meaningful and interesting way. Usually, I will wake up in the course of the night with the solution, which I must write down immediately before it is lost.

Many writers work from character in the knowledge that, once characters are established, they direct the book. PHYLLIS WHITNEY says:

I'm a combination of the writer who makes lots of notes and the one who says "Let's see what happens." I work on my plot and characters in copious notes ahead of time. I keep a section running in my notebook, where I jot down every stray idea that comes to me in connection with the current story, talking to myself on paper as I work things out. These ideas are crossed out as they are used in my plan, or are discarded. When it comes to making an outline, however, I am very spare. The fewest possible words go down to indicate action for each chapter. These set my framework. Within it, I never know exactly what is going to happen or what my characters are going to say and do. They surprise me constantly and keep me entertained while writing. Some of my best effects appear unexpectedly, yet because of all the groundwork I've done, my subconscious is influenced and they fit into the pattern. Extra scenes suggest themselves; sometimes even a new character will walk onstage, and I won't know how I got along without him.

ROSE V. LANNI tells how she works up a character:

Before I even begin, I spend about six weeks making a notebook about my characters — entering background, temperaments, motivations, details of physique, age, lineage, and the like. I also scan magazines and when I see a picture of someone who reminds me of my character, I cut it out and affix it to his "record." By the time I'm done, I know my characters backwards and forwards and the book seems fairly to be writing itself.

GEORGE BROWN MAIR remarks:

I have no method except that I suddenly find myself "tense" and that this tension increases over a few days until there is a compulsion to put down a sentence on paper. Thereafter I write for up to ten hours daily, or as often as I can be at my desk.

EDWARD D. HOCH reaches the same place by a different route:

I work with a few notes on short stories, but with extensive outlines on novels. At the beginning of a project, work might be slow — only a few hours a day, if that much. Toward the end of a story, or in rewriting, I may be at the typewriter throughout the afternoon and evening — some 12 hours at a stretch.

A number of writers specify their use of a spiral notebook, as Patricia Highsmith does, while others prefer filing cards or a clipboard, as if the physical paraphernalia constituted a kind of security blanket.

PAULINE C. SMITH says:

But I must get to the typewriter, somehow, sometime each day, for if I don't, I immediately become limp and rusty. Two days away from the typewriter and I haven't the slightest idea how to start a story — three days away, and I'm not even sure of the keyboard.

JANET GREGORY VERMANDEL tells how switching to a different method of work can be helpful:

I write on an electric typewriter, but I've found that if I'm tired, or stuck at some point in the story, I can get going again by switching to longhand for awhile. One of the most effective tricks I've learned is to sit down with a pad and pen (and a drink, as a reward for virtue) when I'm through for the night, and while my mind is still more or less in gear, write a page or so as a head start on the next day's work. No sweat, if it doesn't work out, you haven't lost anything. But it's astonishing how good it looks to you next day, how much easier it is to get going when you don't have to do it from a standing start.

But writing is hard work, as LAWRENCE KAMARCK points out:

Every page must be read and every inconsistency noted. I find this onerous, horrible, ghastly. The fun of creation is over. If there's any joy left, it's the secret one of discovering that it's possible to justify almost any and all behavior. This is also the time when you (or I) discover the form of the plot, which will now require paring and additions. There goes a month.

Then I spend another month rewriting the whole damn thing, making sure all inconsistencies are gone, the logic of character motivation is faultless, spelling is decent, grammar reasonably decent.

In the heat of hatred, wishing I had never begun, I read the miserable result. All I want to know is, does it work as a book? Will it leave a reader with some iota of feeling toward the idea of the book? Did it *have* an idea? If it has no impact for a reader, I say the hell with it and put it away in the file for a later, more objective reading. I have found that a year will give me that objectivity. Then I'll redo the whole damned thing. If it still doesn't have an impact, I'll put it away for good.

In the meantime, I'll begin something new.

PAULINE BLOOM points out how rugged is the urge to create. She says:

I have written in subways, libraries, on park benches, in museums, while listening to dull speakers, in bus, train and airport waiting rooms. The worst writing conditions were in my own home with five growing girls, each with an over-abundance of friends who were always dropping in, a father who always sang, a radio and piano and telephone always in action, sometimes simultaneously. It was Grand Central Station on Christmas Eve. Only nominally did I have a room of my own, with a door. But I did write.

Miss Bloom's experience reminds me of a scene some years ago in a village in Spain where Bruce Graeme had rented a small, a very small house for the winter. He would sit in a low chair, a pad in his lap, and he'd jot down a phrase, a sentence or two, I never knew exactly what. Meanwhile two young children effervesced, his wife cooked, and two or three friends sampled his carafe of local brandy. Occasionally he'd join in the conversation for a minute or two, and then go back to his work.

The book he was writing? It sold, of course.

It is not, however, a method to recommend. It is far better to have the good working conditions that ROBERT L. FISH advises:

I think one thing should be said for beginning writers — make your writing area comfortable. I have a big desk, with the typewriter ell large enough for lots of papers; my shelf of reference books is directly overhead and properly furnished with foreign language dictionaries, atlases, my indispensable Roget and (much more dispensable) Bartlett, etc. The encyclopedias require my standing up, but what can you do? My hi-fi is next to it, and a radio. I have a comfortable swivel chair, proper lighting on my typewriter, an electric typewriter and a spare. Writing under comfortable conditions, I think, is essential to writing quickly and producing a lot of work. My room is completely isolated from the rest of the house, and since my wife works, I am undisturbed during my working day.

DOROTHY SALISBURY DAVIS, after saying "I try to finish the day on an incomplete section, which makes the next day's starting easier," adds a sentence to which many writers will say *Amen.* "Yes," she says. "I often find writing itself a scourge, and I still believe a story is a miracle."

The miracle, however, does not perform itself. JOE GORES gives us some of the details of his personal miracles:

I write seven hours a day, six days a week. This is the ideal, of course. Interruptions and the daily events of being a human being take their toll. I do a great deal of rewriting, aim for (everything in) about 400,000 to 600,000 words a year on novels, shorts, screen plays, fact books. I sometimes outline, sometimes don't. But because of my notebook system, I usually have notes of some sort before beginning a story. On novels, these notes might run as many as 30 to 40 single-spaced pages, not in outline but merely disjointed notes. Until I've done a first draft, I'm not sure where the book is going.

On short stories, I usually do five type drafts, though I have done as few as three and as many as 16. Each of these is revised extensively with pen before the fresh draft is typed. I can figure between 25,000 and 30,000 words of rough drafting to come up with a 5,000-word short, which is why they take me a long time.

On novels, a 65,000-word mystery will come in

around 90,000 words first draft. I will pare that to about 70,000 to 75,000 on second draft, then will do extensive "paste-in" inserts on that second draft to squeeze out the final 5,000 to 10,000 words. Because I work in drafts, I let several weeks (or months) pass between first and second draft, meanwhile doing a draft of some other book or screen play, or try to first-draft a couple of short stories. I have not written a book on which the first notes were not taken five to ten years before actual work on the text began. The notes, of course, may have nothing to do with what finally emerges. Often I will make notes on an idea and forget about them, then make notes on a second unrelated idea, forget them, make notes on a third idea — and something in my mind makes a connection. I remember those first two ideas, dig them out, combine them, and *voilà!* a novel idea.

Because I believe the plot must grow out of the characters rather than vice versa, all of my books change drastically between conception and completion, as the characters grow, develop, take over during the course of the book. In a mystery this means, after the first draft is done, making up lists of plot points, gimmicks, clues, and the like and making sure they actually turn up in the text.

Also, in the interests of realism, I research backgrounds and legal points and medical points thoroughly, making extensive taped descriptions of locales I will be using, as well as taped descriptions of the weather, the people who live in the area, etc. It takes extra time before you can begin working on the text itself, but it pays off handsomely, I believe, in "hard" detail which helps drag a reader into your story and keep him there.

Do you want to create another Sherlock Holmes, or do you just want to be yourself, with no *alter ego*? The question is an important one, and Hillary Waugh, who has succeeded in both, discusses the problem.

9. The Series vs. the Non-Series Detective

by Hillary Waugh

Now that you are ready to sit down at the typewriter, plot in hand, to write your first mystery novel, one of the questions that faces you is, what are you going to do about your detective? Is he or she to be an ongoing character making his appearance in future books, or is this to be his only case, the book not just wrapping up the murder, but the detective as well? Since one can go either way, the decision to be made is, which way is better, and why?

If money and writing security are your goals — and they usually are — then the series detective seems the best bet. Agatha Christie to the contrary notwithstanding, it can be given as a general rule that fictional detectives are better known than their creators. Agatha Christie is admittedly more of a household name than either Hercule Poirot or Miss Jane Marple, but even Miss Christie's renown pales before that of Sherlock Holmes. Sherlock, the detective we all wish we had invented, not only dwarfs his creator, Sir Arthur Conan Doyle, he dwarfs most real people as well, both past and present, and, in fact, is recognized as the most famous fictional character ever conceived — with the possible exception of Tarzan. In like manner, as well known as such authors as Rex Stout and Erle Stanley Gardner may be, their detectives, Nero Wolfe and Perry Mason, are even better known.

And for a classic example: who in the world has not heard of Charlie Chan? Yet who besides a mystery buff, can name his creator?

The point is that the average mystery reader, when impressed by a particular story, is going to look for more of the same. Same what? More stories about the same detective, of course. It is the detective's name that will stick in his mind. Only incidentally, and as an aid in case the detective's name is not on the book jacket, will he take heed of the author's name.

That being the case, if a writer can create an appealing, intriguing, or interesting detective, there is a definite advantage — both for him and for the mystery reader — in his continuing his detective through further adventures. With each new book, the detective's following, and therefore the author's readership (it's not the other way around, mind you) grow. And as new readers encounter the detective for the first time and like him, they will go back to earlier books to acquaint themselves with his previous exploits. Meanwhile, the reappearance of the detective's name with each new book is akin to advertising the whole package. An author develops something of a legacy, as it were. He assures himself and his publisher of a certain sales expectancy. He is producing a known quantity, and that, in the very uncertain field of publishing, is a decided plus.

With all these desirable advantages, one might well ask why any mystery or detective story writer would ever produce anything but series detectives. Why turn out a one-shot story and never use that particular hero or heroine again? What are the advantages of a non-series story, and what are the disadvantages of the series type?

One disadvantage, believe it or not, is that an author can become tired of his series detective, yet be stuck with him. (Conan Doyle tried his darndest to get rid of Sherlock Holmes, but his public wouldn't let him.) Worse than that, an author may outgrow his series detective and find him a hindrance. What is worst of all, is the author who *fails* to outgrow his detective because he stays loyal to him.

Another disadvantage is the likelihood of the author becoming jaded and losing his fresh approach. Familiarity does breed contempt and sometimes, if the marriage continues too long, the detective can start to become a caricature of *him*self and the author an imitator of *him*self. While series detectives have their purposes and their plus sides, generally speaking it is best if they don't stay around too long.

As for the non-series type of mystery novel, what does it have to offer? What are its advantages?

What is *not* an advantage is the lack of a ready-made audience. Readers, it is true, do at times get to like an author for himself alone. (There is one mystery writer who even has a fan club). Nevertheless, it takes more of a reading connoisseur to fancy an author because of the way he writes rather than because of what he writes. Thus, as a general rule, the audience that picks up a mystery because it's by author A. Good Riter is going to be smaller than the one that picks up a mystery because it's about Detective Derring Do.

On the plus side, these one-shot books offer the author a chance to experiment, to try different ways of telling stories, to try different kinds of stories. Some stories, for example, need to be told in the first person singular, rather than in the traditional third. A different technique is required. If a writer wants to develop himself, he should experiment with and master different techniques. Some stories emphasize action, others suspense, still others mood, dialogue, or drama. There are wide varieties of tales to tell, and they cannot all be explored if an author is tied to a series detective and to an audience that expects the same kind of book from him each time.

Then there is the matter of the degree of involvement of the characters with the story. This is important, for it triggers and determines the reader's degree of involvement. A novel about a young girl setting out to find the murderer of her brother is going to make a very different impact upon the reader than a novel about a young girl asking the series detective to find the murderer of her brother.

In one-shot novels, a degree of involvement with the characters can be developed and sustained that can't be achieved with a series detective. The series detective is an onlooker. The romances, the love affairs, the heartaches and tears, the tragic or happy endings all happen to others. The series detective (and therefore the reader) remains untouched and unchanged, ready to move on to the next case. All the series detective gets from the heroine is a look of heartfelt gratitude as she melts into the waiting arms of the rescued hero. The detective's arms remain empty — or are entered only at great risk. (One author, who let his series detective marry, had to kill off the new wife to sell the series to the movies.)

Which route, then, is the best to take? Should one follow the safe and sane, but ultimately stultifying road of the series character or try the demanding, less certain, but more satisfying path of the one-shot novel? Or should one try, as I have done several times over, switching back and forth, and become neither fish nor fowl?

A friend who cut his writing teeth on a paperback-original series-character but who now writes hard-cover straight novels, says he sometimes thinks of his long-ago detective as sitting in his office somewhere waiting for a next case.

Other things being equal, like tastes, inclinations, needs and abilities, perhaps his is the best route for the beginning writer: start with a series character, learn with him, build with him, and then, when you outgrow him, leave him in his office waiting for that next case, and move on to the next stage of your own career.

Police work is at the bottom of most crime stories, but few of us know enough about it. Too often we repeat statements we've read or heard without realizing how inaccurate they are. Surely the primary responsibility of every writer is to tell the truth and to avoid perpetuating myths that earlier writers have started. Are you aware, for instance, that fingerprints are rarely found on the steering wheel of a car (your fingers slide off the wheel and at best leave only a smudge), and practically never on the oily trigger of a handgun?

Thomas M. McDade, lawyer, writer, Edgar winner, former F.B.I. agent, and head of a corporate security department, details crime procedures and assorted facts that you ought to know, and he interlards them with some fascinating anecdotes from his personal experience.

10. Homicide and Other Investigations

by Thomas M. McDade

For anyone who has watched television courtroom dramas or police stories in which errors of law or police procedure regularly appear the question must arise: How important is it to be exact in such matters as the correct rules of evidence or legal procedure? The Perry Mason series abounded in improper legal tactics, despite the fact that it was written or conceived by a very successful criminal lawyer who knew what he was about. How do you argue with such success?

For the amateur I can only suggest that if you intend to depart from the rules, you should know how and why you are doing it. Errors of ignorance seem to point a finger at incompetence, but deliberate departure for the sake of dramatic impact may be excusable. Watching a courtroom play in which the lawyers had to follow the real rules of evidence would be a dreadful bore. So I suggest that, no matter how many questionable tactics or ploys you see other writers use and get away with, you should know what is right and what is wrong and choose the latter only if you have a good reason for doing so. Moreover, the reading and viewing public are so much more sophisticated today about courtroom and police procedure, from press and TV exposure, that errors or omissions are more likely to be recognized.

The following comments are offered on the major questions a writer must face in writing a detective or mystery story in which the organization and role of the police or some governmental agency, the scientific information pertinent to the case, or trial and legal procedures are important to the story.

Police Organization. For someone planning to write police procedurals, like the Ed McBain or Gideon series, little that will be said here will help. For such a task nothing short of almost total familiarity with the department's operations will be adequate to the task. And such familiarity comes only from the inside.

Police departments vary widely from city to city — even titles do not mean the same thing. What, for instance, is an inspector? On the homicide squad in San Diego he's a working detective, but in New York City he is a high ranking executive. A police sergeant in New York is a technical man versed in procedure: he runs the station house switchboard, dispatches and channels complaints. He is the strawboss of the uniformed force. What a sergeant does in any of the other major cities, I would have to conjecture, and it doesn't pay to guess.

The point I am making is that if your book is plotted in an identified city or town, you will have to acquaint yourself with such details of organization. This is not as difficult as it sounds, but it will take some legwork as there are no written materials to explain the organization. Large metropolitan departments like Los Angeles or New York, however, will have a public relations office where a writer can get help on the details, organization and procedures of the department. In asking for such help describe yourself as a free-lance writer — even if you have never been published — police never mind talking to professionals; amateurs make them uneasy.

The mechanics and the titles used in other government agencies such as the Federal Bureau of Narcotics, the F.B.I., the Naturalization and Immigration Service and the State

Police, all differ. So in describing any of these organizations, if you want an air of authenticity, it can only be attained by a fairly close contact with the unit itself.

Just as functions have different names, departments and localities have their own argot. Beware of slang and underworld speech; it can be a real trap. The uninitiated will use terms which to the informed sound like a foreigner speaking from a dictionary. For an example of the right way to handle underworld speech, read *The Friends of Eddie Coyle,* by George V. Higgins, whose ear for the nuances and expressions of Massachusetts barroom conversation gives exceptional authenticity to the scenes he creates.

Medical Examiner, Coroner and the Cause of Death. The morgue of old with its shrouded figures lying on wheeled tables in a large tiled room survives today only in late show horror films. Now, as we all know, cadavers are stored in refrigerated lockers with small doors, until a skilled staff of medical experts including pathologists, toxicologists, and others converge on the corpse and anatomize it, the head doctor meanwhile loudly dictating his report as he wields his scalpel: "This is the body of a well-nourished white male, seventy-two and one-quarter inches long and weighing one hundred seventy-five pounds." Perhaps some social scientist can find some significance in the fact that all our homicide victims are well-nourished; for myself the use of that term always distracted me from the more important scientific finding that usually followed.

Either by a medical examiner or coroner, the cause of death must be established in every case where the deceased has not been attended by a physician who can certify the cause of death. Bodies remain at the place where found until a member of that office releases it, and in the case of a violent death it is usually taken to the mortuary where a postmortem or autopsy is conducted. In a large city the medical examiner's office has skilled scientists available in all the fields of forensic medicine, and his opinion on the cause of death is generally very difficult to dispute.

Not all communities, however, have such elaborate facilities for conducting autopsies, and the Frankenstein tradition may not be entirely lost to the modern world. Quite a few years ago, while working out of the F.B.I.'s Miami office, I got a call from a sheriff in central Florida who was concerned about the death of a lighthouse keeper on the St. John's River. The body had been found floating in the river and, as I learned when I visited the town, had been in the water about ten days, and then buried a week before I arrived, with no autopsy performed. Disorder found in the lighthouse raised questions about the death, however, and since the lighthouse was a government installation on federal property, any crime committed there would be a federal offense.

My first step was to get an autopsy performed, since I had no basis for investigation until cause of death could be established. My first difficulty was in procuring a doctor who would agree to do it, and when I finally found one, the town health officer refused to let the body be brought back into town because of the health hazard. The macabre scene at the graveside lacked only Boris Karloff and drifting fog. The enormously bloated body, never embalmed, had been buried in the outer case of a coffin, the coffin itself being too small. The lid of the case, on a trestle of sawhorses, was our operating table. The surgeon stoically declined the smoke mask I had borrowed from the fire department to avoid the stench, but went about his task as quickly as possible. Fortunately, he was able to establish that there were no skull injuries and that death was due to dislocation of the neck; he had apparently fallen accidentally from the lighthouse into shallow water, striking a sandy bottom and snapping his vertebra.

The moral of this tale is that despite the profound and wide-ranging scientific advances in forensic medicine, they are not yet universally available. Let mystery writers fit the quality of the services to the community in which the crime takes place.

Informers. The word "informer" conjures up the image of a furtive, skulking figure, met in shadowy alleys, who in fear and trembling, whispers where so-and-so can be found or who did that last heist. You shove a few dollars in his hands, and he disappears into the shadows, only to be found dead in a drab rooming house two chapters later. Undoubtedly there are such types, but the description only shows how we tend to stereotype all characters and reduce them to a formula. Personally I never met one who quite fit that description.

There is no doubt about the enormous value of a good informer, or informant, as such sources are generally called today. With the possible exception of drug groups, police officers cannot infiltrate a criminal gang. The criminal history of each member is well known to his associates; his background is as carefully authenticated as a job applicant's resumé. "Woodville Farm, Monterey Correctional Camp, Elmira Reformatory, Edgecomb Rehabilitation Center, Great Meadows Correctional Facility, Clinton Correctional Facility (Dannemora)" — so the roster runs. Thus information must come to the detective either from a member of the gang, or, more likely, a peripheral hanger-on.

A detective's success will depend, in large measure, on the sources he can develop close to criminals. For information he usually barters freedom rather than money. Most police departments have very limited funds for buying information, but the favors they can confer by way of immunity from prosecution for other transgressions are more than a match for money.

It is more difficult for the private investigator to get informants. Years ago I asked Charlie Scaffa, once one of the great private detectives in this country, how he got his. Many of them came to his attention in a minor case, and he recognized that they would someday be useful. He would keep in touch with them, finance them over trying periods and then press them into service when a big case arose. On the other hand, he told me, they sometimes sought him out. One day an ex-con walked into his office, still in prison suit and shoes and asked for a loan of $100. Charlie lent him the money on the strength of his heavy criminal background, the grounds most of us would have used for refusing. About a month later, he saw the same man drive by in a new Cadillac, dressed in a tailor-made suit. And three months later, Charlie's investment paid off. The day after a valuable truckload of furs was hijacked, Charlie got a call from the man inquiring whether he was interested in the case. Scaffa told him he represented the insurance company, and the man told him: "The truck is in a garage on Bay 13th street, Brooklyn," and gave him the number. For Scaffa's original $100 investment, he recovered a $75,000 load of furs.

Unfortunately the one thing you rely on in an informant is his eventual unreliability. His first offering is usually good, but on the strength of this he keeps coming back for more money. Since he doesn't have much to sell, sooner or later, he begins inventing tales.

Police Science in General. Basic to a good crime story is an understanding of the science of criminalistics, a term which includes all the scientific techniques applied to criminal investigations. The following pages are not intended to acquaint the reader with the basic scientific facts in the categories given. Instead, I make suggestions as to how this information may best be used, mention pitfalls to avoid, and give some illustrations from cases which may help to stimulate other ideas on the subject.

Firearms. As with other scientific evidence, if you are not really familiar with guns, be careful how you use them in your story. Get some person knowledgeable in weapons to check out your details. But, as with all bodies of scientific data, it is the quirks, the oddities of a subject which can be used for misdirection. For example, a bullet hole found in the windshield of a car through which you could not pass a .38 calibre bullet would suggest that it was fired from a weapon of smaller calibre. Not generally known, however, is that when a bullet passes through certain kinds of glass, the glass bends, permitting a slug to go through, but then returning to a size through which the same bullet could not be re-passed.

Recently there was a flurry of criticism of the use of dumdum bullets by a State Police force, since they are outlawed by the international rules of war. A dumdum (named after the town in India where first made) has either a hollow point or a deep cut in the soft lead nose so that the slug shatters on impact and tears a large hole by reason of its tumbling action. It can make a dreadful wound, particularly when it exits from the body, and its use today has generally been confined to hunting game. And yet I owe my life to the fact that when a fugitive fired at me with a rifle, he used dumdums. He fired out of an automobile through his car windshield: the lead slugs mushroomed when they hit the glass, lost their shape and velocity, and were spent on impact with the car in which I was riding.

Beware, also, of the temptation to make use of bizarre homemade contrivances. It's technically possible to fire a .32 calibre bullet from a modified .38 calibre gun, but such tricks introduce the improbable into a story trying to comport with a real life situation. Unless your operator is an expert in the use of firearms, he probably couldn't do it, and such tricks as the opening of locked doors with hairpins are also more feats of legerdemain than practical procedures.

Older books on investigation mention the paraffin test, used to determine whether a person had recently fired a pistol. Soft paraffin was applied to a suspect's hand to remove any particles of gunpowder and then tested chemically. It was a very uncertain test and has now been superseded by the highly sophisticated neutron-activation analysis machine, a much more sensitive and reliable testing device. Developed for an entirely different purpose, the machine has detected even very minute particles of burnt gunpowder on the hands, and its test results have been admitted in evidence.

James Bond has helped to make the foreign automatic pistol into a popular weapon for sleuths, and, of course, a shoulder holster is *de rigueur*. But few police officers would be found with an automatic, mainly because of the double hazard of carrying the weapon cocked and the possibility that it will jam when the cartridge case ejects. The .38 calibre detective special with its short (two inch) barrel is more trustworthy, safer, and is generally worn on the belt. A few of the younger men do affect a second gun, chiefly when working under cover, which they may wear in an ankle holster.

Wiretapping, Voiceprint and Polygraph. Revelations about official and unofficial bugging in the past couple of years should make anything said now on the subject a bit redundant; besides, the simplicity of a mere telephone tap hardly intrigues the imagination.

Of more interest today are the new highly developed directional microphones, voice activated, which pick up conversations previously considered impossible to monitor. Today, spy stories abound with feats of listening to and recording the conversation of two people whispering in the middle of an empty football stadium with the help of a parabolic directional microphone. The only problem is, it would require the resources of a large government department; your average gumshoe couldn't afford it.

One of the more recently developed instruments involving voice recording is a machine to identify the speaker as positively as people are identified by fingerprints. Appropriately enough it is called a voiceprint, and the device makes a graphic picture of the human voice when it is fed a speech sample recorded on tape. The machine used to do this, a sound spectograph, has been in use in medicine to record and analyze body sounds, such as heart, lungs, etc. It is essentially an automatic sound wave analyzer.

The character of individual speech is determined by the size, shape, and position of the vocal cavities in the mouth and throat, and by the lips, tongue, palate, etc. It is claimed that human variability in these factors makes it impossible for these voices to be identical.

The machine produces a graph-like recording on a sheet of paper, and only a skilled operator can compare one such recording with another and make an identification. There is presently a conflict in the courts on the admissibility of such evidence; a considered review of the legal and scientific opinion on the subject will be found in the case of U.S. v. Addison, 498 F. 2d 741 (1974).

The so-called lie detector, or polygraph, relies on the simultaneous measurement of blood pressure, respiration, and a galvanic measurement of skin resistance, the last being the least reliable. The secret of good polygraph testing lies in the skill of the operator. Simply putting a suspect on the "box" and asking a long series of questions does not produce results. The theory is that after a very short space of time the subject loses his psychic elasticity, and it becomes increasingly difficult to differentiate between truthful answers and lies.

Fingerprints. The serious use of fingerprints in a mystery has become almost obsolete, probably because almost every trick on the subject has been exploited. Nonetheless, the crime scene is routinely "dusted" for latent prints, and suspects have their prints taken to be matched with any found. Spray guns and fuming kits have replaced camel's hair brushes, and dragon's blood and other exotic-sounding dusting powders are now passé. However, new scientific discoveries have made possible the detection of fingerprints on materials where before it was uncertain at best and in many cases impossible. Ninhydrin can now make prints on paper where iodine fumes once produced blotches, and this chemical has even developed fingerprints thirty years old.

The most common misunderstanding about fingerprints is that a single latent print found at a crime scene can be checked against the general fingerprint files. It usually can't, because fingerprints are sorted under a system requiring prints of all ten fingers. A few major police departments and the F.B.I. have a single fingerprint file, but those prints are limited to a small number of major criminals such as kidnappers and bank robbers. In short, you can only compare a single latent fingerprint with those of a known suspect.

I was once fingerprinting a man in North Carolina whom we had arrested and was rolling each finger out on to the card which had the usual two rows of five squares, one for each finger. The operator holds the hand and rolls each finger in turn beginning with the thumb. Suddenly I found myself holding a finger ready to apply it to the square on the card, but the square wasn't there. I looked at the card, baffled for a moment, but it wasn't my equipment that was faulty: the man had six fingers on each hand.

Another common misconception is that the wearing of gloves confers complete protection from leaving marks at a crime scene. Some kinds of gloves, particularly leather, have their own pattern of lines and creases, which can sometimes leave marks as clearly identifiable as fingerprints, and this is more likely with old wrinkled gloves that have acquired a film of dirt or grease to leave a mark.

Alteration of fingerprints makes poor fiction and worse fact. Actually fingerprints have been obliterated by surgery so that the pattern which made the original fingerprint classification has disappeared and the classification cannot be reconstructed from the scarred fingers. One major confidence man had his prints removed by surgery, and when he was

arrested in a western state on suspicion, he could not be identified in the limited time he could be held in jail without
a charge against him. About a week after his release the identification was effected in Washington but he had already disappeared and it was a year or two before he again came
into custody. By then a separate file of such obliterated prints
had been established and he was easily identified.

Perhaps the most significant new development in the fingerprint area has to do with the automation of the searching
process through files containing records of millions of people.
Such automation, of course, would greatly reduce the time
and cost of processing a set of prints. The F.B.I. is presently
inaugurating a plan known as the "Automated Identification
Division System" (the acronym is AIDS), which will eventually provide for automatic fingerprint searching, computerized
name searching of criminal name indices, computer storage
and retrieval of arrest data and the capability of gathering
criminal statistics at the same time.

Rigor Mortis. As with fingerprints, rigor mortis has gotten
less attention in recent fiction because little that's new can
be said about it. The writer now makes the usual courtesy
acknowledgment that the phenomenon was observed and an
opinion expressed on when the death took place. The basic
facts are these: between one and six hours after death, usually
starting at the face and head and moving downward, the
body begins to stiffen. This stiffening is caused by the coagula-
tion of muscle protein and plasma, and when the process
is complete, the forced movement of an arm or leg can create
a detectable tear in muscle tissue. The rigidity lasts from
twelve to forty-eight hours, after which it diminishes and finally disappears. There are so many variables in the whole
process (temperature at the location of the body, degree of
physical activity the victim had engaged in just before death,
etc.) that the observed symptoms and conditions can merely
help the investigator to make a rough estimate of the time

of death; it is just one factor to be considered along with other evidence pointing to the time of death.

Surveillance. What was once quaintly known as "shadowing," and is now generally referred to as "tailing," is much more difficult than most people imagine. The new realism in television police programs suggests some of the problems, but the picture of the chief directing a dozen cars by radio to keep in touch with a car they are following is still highly idealized.

The problem falls in two parts. If the person being followed is not suspicious and is not looking for a tail, the difficulties are minimal, but not entirely non-existent. If the person *is* watching for a tail, then the difficulties are substantial, and tactics will be determined by whether the follower cares if he is "made." Russian agents are followed continuously in American cities; they expect it. The F.B.I. usually assigned two surveillance teams per subject, each team consisting of a radio-equipped automobile, a driver, and two "footmen." Some of the surveillances in Manhattan were particularly difficult because of traffic conditions. As the surveillance progressed, they sometimes left a trail of irate cabbies and insulted pedestrians.

On foot surveillance, if three men were available, one usually positioned himself about half a block behind the subject on the same side of the street.The second man was stationed about a block behind the first man, also on the same side of the street. The third man was about a block behind the subject on the other side of the street. The "footmen" kept changing places, and the distance behind the subject varied, of course, with the surroundings. On a lonely street it was necessary to keep several blocks between yourself and the subject. In crowds, it was necessary to move up very close to avoid losing contact.

A typical day-long surveillance provided a series of dilemmas, the first, and continuing one, being, had we been "made"? Decisions had to be made instantly. — Should a member of the team get on the elevator with the subject? Was the subject going to get on the subway, or was he going to try to "dry clean" himself by getting on, then jumping off just as the doors were closing? I recall one Russian agent who lost us by walking into Central Park, and then jogging briskly across the terrain. Anyone jogging after him was obviously following. Another subject walked into Central Park, went around a corner, and lay down in a drainage ditch. The surveillance team came hightailing it along, and one-by-one jumped over him. It must have looked like a steeplechase.

I am always surprised at the ease with which suspects are tailed on television. The hero correctly interprets the subject's action, anticipates what he will do next, takes a shortcut, and catches up with him. In my experience, that kind of cuteness has lost many subjects. We once lost a prominent Russian "illegal" whom we had been following for months because we thought we knew his habits. We stopped about a block from his apartment house, while he passed it, took a cab from the next corner, and was never seen again. Mr. Hoover was terribly displeased.

Surveillance on a site—a meeting place or a drop for the delivery of some object—can be a long and frustrating experience. But frustration is the alchemy of the writer who can use it to add color and suspense to his tale. I have sat for untold hours watching a package full of torn newspaper in hopes that the extortionist would pick it up. I saw dogs piss on it, drunks pick it up while poring through trash baskets, children come by and use it for a football, kicking it off down the street in front of them. Once we actually had to fight with a drunk to retrieve the package, as he was sure he had found something valuable and thought we were trying to do him out of it.

Courts and Trials. Questions of law should be treated with respect. The writer should have some basic knowledge of criminal law and, if he introduces a courtroom scene, of the rules of evidence. Furthermore, he should be familiar with the different degrees of murder in whatever jurisdiction he sets his crime. With the recent wave of new laws on the subject, it is best to consult a lawyer friend for their current status. For a while in New York, for instance, there were no degrees of murder; then, following the Furman decision, first degree murder was reestablished with a mandatory death penalty.

The unending stream of television courtroom dramas has educated almost everyone in the rudiments of the criminal justice system. The problem of the writer is not in learning the details, but in using them with dramatic effect and avoiding excessive attention to matters which do not advance the story. Whatever details are selected should aid in character or plot development.

An understanding of the fundamentals of courtroom procedure and a few rules of evidence is easily procured from books and articles, but a day or two in your local court watching a trial will pay better dividends. You are bound to observe small incidents which will be useful to you in creating live, convincing trial scenes. If possible, visit the detention pens from which the defendants who are not on bond are brought before a judge. In some New York City courts, these resemble zoos: on a floor below the court prisoners are held in cages not unlike animal cages, and an attorney may have to discuss the case with his client through the bars of a cubicle made to hold two persons, but which is actually holding eight or ten.

One problem the writer may face has to do with the questioning of medical or other expert witnesses. The safest guide in this area is the transcript of an actual trial in which comparable evidence was given. Your local bar association library may have reference books which give examples of such testimony. In many cities, the major court for the district also has a library which has such books, and the librarian can be very helpful.

A work of imposing dimensions, *Courtroom Medicine,* edited by Marshall Houts, consists of twenty separate volumes covering testimony about injuries and ailments to every part of the body. Three volumes alone are devoted to the subject of death, and they include a detailed description of an autopsy. Of interest to the writer are citations of the actual cases the material is taken from, with copious examples of questions and answers in the examination of medical witnesses.

Some court libraries have on file a copy of the trial transcript of most of the cases which were appealed. If the writer knows of a case in which a certain expert testified (on blood stains, hair, fingerprints, etc.) and the conviction was appealed, he may be able to locate the testimony in this way. In New York City all cases which went to the Appellate Division, the court to which all appeals of felony cases are taken, are on file at the bar association library.

In most states, a general digest of cases exists to help you find the sort of testimony you need. In New York it is "Abbotts Digest," in which cases are organized by subject. The official decision of the case on appeal also gives the name and city of the attorney of record for the defendant on appeal. It is often possible to borrow the trial transcript from the attorney to use as a guide in writing the court testimony in a story.

Jails and Prisons. So much has been written in the past few years about jail and prison conditions that you may consider yourself well-informed on the subject. I have found from experience that no two people see the same thing, or if they do, interpret it in the same way. I can only repeat that there is no substitute for personal experience. An hour spent in a place of confinement will provide more color and detail than a dozen books or articles.

Visit your local jail; there are always community groups

doing so. And visit your nearest prison, or correctional facility, as they prefer to call them today. Modern penologists are trying to get communities involved in prison affairs; they feel that the isolation of the prisoner from the community hinders his rehabilitation. Note each step of the processing you will receive on first entering: each turn of a key, the clothes worn, the questions asked. After your first visit, set down immediately everything observed. Count the locked doors you passed through; describe the package searches; list the items in your pockets you were not allowed to take in with you (your pills must usually be left at the desk). It may startle you to see so many inmates moving freely about the inside of the prison, and so few guards, but there are other things as well. On my first visit at one institution, I was crossing the prison yard among 400 inmates, and was struck by the number of cats prowling about; there were literally dozens. Somehow cats seem to be tolerated in many prisons, but I have never seen a dog inside.

Be warned. We quickly grow blasé, and what took us by surprise on first sight will pass unnoticed a second or third time. Capture that surprise; it is what will give your reader the same interest and excitement it gave you when first you saw it.

Ellery Queen states: "There is no short-cut, no royal road, to quick and enduring success. The writing game is full of heartache and heartbreak. The only sure formula for success can be stated in simple terms: talent and indomitable perseverance — and one is almost valueless without the other . . . . Sure it's tough, and every editor with a heart can say with absolute truth that when he returns a manuscript it hurts him more than it hurts the writer — especially if the editor is himself a writer."

Eleanor Sullivan is such an editor. She has worked at Pocket Books and Scribner's, and is now managing editor of *Ellery Queen's Mystery Magazine.*

In this article she goes into the nitty-gritty of submitting, and in the course of it, she reflects the general attitude of an intelligent and sensitive editor.

11. How to Please an Editor

by Eleanor Sullivan

If you don't see any particular reason for pleasing an editor beyond writing a first-rate manuscript whose length and subject matter suit his needs, you would do well to skip this chapter because (1) you are right, and (2) chances are that if you can write a first-rate manuscript and know the market, you have also divined the basic do's and don'ts of manuscript submission.

In preparing this chapter, I asked several leading mystery editors for their advice regarding the approach a new writer should take in sending material to them. In his response, Don Bensen spoke of editorial variables that are beyond the writer's control. What the writer can control, however, Don says, "is not bugging the editor. Double-spaced typescript, one side of the paper, and so on . . . ."

And, he says, "junk or trade in that typewriter with the fancy script face — the page is not supposed to *look* interesting, but to read that way. Do not, in the covering letter or on the title page, claim that your manuscript is covered by statutory copyright or registered with a trusted friend — most editors will assume that if you're that suspicious to start with, you will, in the event of being offered a contract, take it to an attorney specializing in leases who will decorate it with a lacework of rewording and extra clauses which will create headaches for the contract department and probably get the deal cancelled. The time to start distrusting your editor and publisher is on your second book — and for that, get an agent and let him do the distrusting, at which he is a pro.

"In working on a book under contract, either keep your deadline or, as soon as you see you're not going to make it, let your editor know about it and ask for a specific extension. That way, he is doing you a favor by granting it — if he has to call up and ask for the book and get evasive answers, he's cast as a heavy, and that makes him feel grim, and unpleased enough to think wistfully of rejecting your next.

"It seems to boil down," Don concludes, "to write like a best-selling angel, but in the details of presentation of manuscript and other routine stuff, be totally and responsibly businesslike."

While, on the one hand, I am constantly amazed at the number of perfectly typed and presented manuscripts that come into the editorial offices where I've worked, I am, on the other hand, appalled by the self-defeating ways in which new writers sometimes present their work.

I once received a letter from an unpublished writer saying that one of the serious obstacles young writers face is the overwhelming lack of consistency in manuscript standards, that the method of approach considered correct by one editor too often contradicts that set by another. The writer was attempting to correct this by way of an enclosed questionnaire, which I consulted eagerly, only to find the questions in the survey of such triviality that I can't believe they have ever been a source of disagreement between editors. The color of the envelope. Stamp preference (U.S. flag, commemorative, novelty, no preference). Form of addressing the envelope — typed? felt-tip marker, printed? felt-tip marker, longhand? Did additional markings such as seals, decals or wax effect [sic] an editor's opinion? In which order should material be placed in the envelope — letter, ms., then SASE? ms., SASE, then letter? SASE, letter, then ms.? Another combination thereof?

Please, dear beginning writer, don't be concerned with these things or think for a minute that editors are. There are subtleties that can jar, but you'd be surprised at what will be overlooked if the manuscript is right. Some general guidelines that may be of help to you in presenting yourself well to an editor are:

An awareness of the market. Sending a short story to a book editor or a novel to a magazine that publishes only short stories is a great waste of time and postage and can make an editor wonder where the author's mind is. This is especially true when the writer lives in a city with easy access to libraries, bookstores, and magazine stands. Anyone with access to the editor's address should at least be aware of what the editor is publishing.

A presentable manuscript, typed, double-spaced, with fairly roomy margins, on standard 8½ x 11 paper. It is well to start your copy halfway down the first page because, in the happy event it is published, the editor will need that space for his instructions to the printer. Although it is not mandatory to do so, it is a kindness to the editor to have a separate title page in case the title is changed, and to give an approximate word count at the top right-hand corner of the first page. Typos and misspellings indicate a lack of literacy or caring that can't help but put an editor on his guard. To the degree that you have control over your typewriter, the manuscript should be clean. Recycling is no excuse for the condition of some manuscripts and SASEs writers send out.

Self-addressed stamped envelopes. Writers are generally pretty good about including them with their manuscripts, realizing that a publisher can't be expected to absorb the cost of returning unsolicited material. When submitting a manuscript to a publisher outside your country, however, your own government's stamps cannot be used in returning the manuscript, so enclose postal-reply coupons (available at any post office) instead. Your return envelope, as well as the one in which you send your manuscript to the editor, should be appropriate to the size of the manuscript. I hate having to mutilate a manuscript to fold it into an envelope too small for it, or to send it swimming back in an envelope too large for its best protection. Strangely enough, those who err most where SASEs are concerned are those who either send their stories heavily wrapped and insured, or deliver them to the publisher's office personally. If you have occasion to do the latter, incidentally, do *not* ask to see the editor in order to discuss the manuscript. It's a cliché, but worth repeating, that what you have written should speak for itself (as it will have to if it's published), and if the editor is doing his job, he will be too busy to see you. It is a situation where he will feel, as Mr. Bensen says, like a heavy — and therefore a situation to avoid. No matter what you feel may be gained by meeting an editor, chances are under these circumstances it won't be worth it.

Multiple submissions. Other editors may feel differently, but generally I think manuscripts should be submitted individually for best psychological effect. If both manuscripts are smashingly good, of course the editor will be delighted; but if one is better than the other, the other may be overlooked — and if they are both below average the editor's negative reaction could infect his attitude toward the author's work in general.

Lost manuscripts. Editors have the greatest sympathy in the world for lost manuscripts and will do all they can to track one down — which unfortunately is difficult to do if it has never reached the office or has been returned in the author's SASE. You should not be timid about querying an editor once a reasonable period of time has elapsed since it was mailed. (Six weeks is a reasonable period.) Do address your to-and-from envelopes accurately and legibly so that the manuscript doesn't wind up in some off-the-beaten-path dead-letter office, impossible to trace. And keep a copy of any and every manuscript you send out. I don't know one author who hasn't had one lost in the mail at some time in his career.

Covering letters. These are by no means necessary. If there is one gesture I especially admire from never-before-published writers submitting to *Ellery Queen's Mystery Magazine,* it is an attached slip of paper or a notation on the title page of the manuscript saying merely: Department of First Stories. This tells me they know the magazine, they know the story must stand on its own, they assume (correctly) that if we are interested in buying the story, we will consult them about payment and any biographical information we need — in other words, that although they have not previously had any fiction published, they have a professional attitude.

Which is not to say that covering letters are not welcome. It is just that too often such letters betray a disorganization or naiveté that is carried through to the accompanying manuscripts. Should you prefer to send a letter with your submission, the following list of things to avoid will help:

Do not say that your ms. has been rejected by another publisher.

Do not plead with the editor to buy your ms. because you need the money.

Do not misname the category in which your manuscript falls — a short story is not an article, for example.

Do not quote an asking price. (Though feel free to ask about rates.)

Do not say that you will abide by the editor's decision or claim that the main characters are figments of your imagination.

Do not hard-sell your work or say your friends think it's excellent.

Do not scold the editor for his policy of not being responsible for unsolicited manuscripts or tell him you think your manuscript is as good as, if not better than, those he has published.

Do not greet him by first name if you've never met him, or as "Dear Person."

Do not ask him to have patience in reading your manuscript because the end is the best part.

Do not have stationery with a letterhead that designates you as Writer or Author.

Do not include a letter of recommendation from anyone who is not a friend of the editor or well known in publishing, or a checklist for the editor to return with your work judging it (1) trite, (2) boring, (3) needs to be rewritten, etc.

Avoid ending your letter with a sad cliché. "Enclosed is a SASE I hope you won't have to use." "I hope you enjoy reading my story as much as I enjoyed writing it." Or something feeble like "Well, enough of this chit-chat." A recent accompanying letter ending "This is a lousy letter, isn't it? All my letters are" was endearing but not very confidence-inspiring.

Don't try to be funny. "I was born eighteen slim years ago in North Pigsty, PA. My hobbies are molesting children and writing. I certainly hope you will buy this or get your throat cut" is neither confidence-inspiring nor endearing.

Finally, don't ask (1) for advice about where else you might send your manuscript if it's rejected (again, it's your business to know the market), (2) for criticism of the manuscript, or (3) whether the editor thinks you have a future in writing. If he expresses interest in your story or buys it you might get into these matters with him, but in the meantime it is not for him to say. You will have to follow your own instincts and the advice of teachers and others whose opinion you respect. I happen to think that you have a great deal more to learn from asking an editor why he wants to buy your story than why he doesn't. Editors' needs vary greatly, and one editor's criticism can needlessly discourage or confuse a new writer to the extent that he might ruin a manuscript for another editor who would have found it perfectly good as it was.

"I have no particular needs or taboos," says Joan Kahn of Harper & Row. "All I want is the freshest, most exciting, best-written, and most believable book an author can do. It can go in any direction it chooses otherwise. And, of course, I'd like it typed double-spaced and I hope the author will have reread it himself at least once before he asks me to read it. And I prefer to see the whole manuscript, not sample chapters with an outline (and an outline without the book's ending *is no outline*)."

"The freshest, most exciting, best-written and most believable book an author can do." It's a tall order. Yet we all have read authors who can handle credible action, dialogue, character, suspense, description and feeling with the agility of a good short-order cook. When I began editing, and read manuscripts that were tired, as far too many are, I concluded that the writers should read more in the field so that they wouldn't embarrass themselves and waste their time on old plots. But I came to realize that, rather than reading too little in the field, these authors were reading too much and relying for direction on what had already succeeded. How much more satisfying it is for an editor (and the readers who buy what he buys) to come across a writer who has an original idea and goes with it, even if it fails.

There are no real taboos as far as story material goes at G. P. Putnam's Sons, Marcia Magill says, except for certain espionage stories. "The spies — either middle-aged and sad-eyed or James Bond-sexy — and the inevitable double and triple crosses all seem stale, even silly, in this post-Cold War era. Of course, Watergate may do wonders for these stories, but at the moment they're harder to sell than the capers and gothics.

"No other taboos, but a few hearty dislikes: stories told in the first person *unless skillfully handled.* These too often sink into an unhappy swamp of pseudo-psychological meanderings, or limit the narrator to scenes in which he *has* to appear. Also, mysteries with too much dialogue and not enough activity, or vice versa.

"As far as protagonists go, we've done extremely well with some very unusual figures: an Indianapolis private eye, a chef, a black chief of police in the Caribbean Islands, a gypsy detective, a little old lady con artist. We've become a little tired of the straight private eyes, even more of the innocent citizen detective, the inquisitive old lady who just happens to pass her parlor curtains and see . . . .

"Occasionally we're asked to gaze in to our crystal ball and predict future trends in mysteries. One thing that's clear to me is that everyone seems to love the evil horror story these days. Mysteries, gothics, suspense novels — anything with a touch of the macabre, the occult, the bizarre seems to find an immediate and enthusiastic audience."

Which brings us back to the bad business of an author requesting criticism from an editor returning a rejected manuscript. *EQMM* readers don't like unmixed horror, and so we usually avoid it. Would it then be fair to come down hard on a story because it's grotesque when there is a thriving market for it elsewhere? When a rejection slip states that a manuscript doesn't suit the publisher's present needs, you can pretty well trust that to be true.

It is a unique and interdependent relationship, this one between author and editor, and it relies heavily on the ability of each to empathize with the other, to put himself squarely into the other's shoes. There is not only a great mutual need to do that but, if it can be achieved, a great mutual admiration that will always lighten the way.

In the earlier edition of this book, Barbara Frost not only pointed out that it's important to be accurate, but she suggested how to go about it. I reprint her chapter in full.

12. How to Make It Authentic

by Barbara Frost

Why bother so much making it authentic? Will they really know the difference? Why not just guess?

I can see it now, that movie a few years ago. Not a bad picture at all – until they came to the big scene. There he was, the struggling young author who had finally made the grade, shaking hands with the editor who had just accepted his book. There they stood in the publisher's office. The beaming editor gazed at the manuscript lying on his desk – completely, utterly unedited, and fully as thick as the Kinsey Report. He then thrust a contract at the young author and uttered these immortal words: "Fine, Mr. So-and-So! Just sign your name, and *we'll have your book in the stall in two weeks!*"

This howler laid in the aisles anyone with even a rudimentary knowledge of the book business. I tottered weakly from the cinema. Later, though, I thought about it as follows: "You happen to know book publishing, and the travel business, because you've worked in those fields. Well, who might your readers be? Steam fitters, concert pianists, botanists, clothing manufacturers, college professors, auto mechanics, doctors, lawyers, TV technicians, theatrical directors, people who train dogs for show, or whatever. Those people know their business or profession. Never forget it!"

But not so easy, you say. How can a writer find out what he needs to know? How soak in facts, procedure, atmosphere, trade talk, reasons why—in short, the feel of what he's writing about, so it will seem not merely correct, but natural, to people who know? They certainly will know, if that field happens to be their own!

The writer has, in general, three ways of setting out to learn how to "make it authentic": books, personal observations and asking people who *do* know.

First, books. Mystery writers need—obviously—more specialized knowledge in certain fields than the average fiction writer, and for them reference books are a Must with a large capital M.

Second, observation—your own. Don't guess—go there, if you can, and find out! Study the lay of the land, the whole procedure. To take a personal example, the background of my first mystery novel, *The Unwelcome Corpse,* was the Washington Square Outdoor Art Show. Like other New Yorkers, I'd enjoyed visiting that show in the spring, but I now had to learn a lot more—the complete layout, how the artists participated, how they actually set the show up, what it was like in different weathers. Furthermore, for purposes of the plot, I had to know every inch of the Park and the adjoining streets as well as you know your own living room.

If your background is a well-known place, you'll want to visit it some more, no matter how well you think you know it. It has back streets, as well as its more famous facade. No matter what your special locale—to make it real to you as well as your readers, you'll want to know the back streets too.

Much of your research will be homely stuff you can do on your own premises. For example, mine has ranged from leaving several different kinds of paper in a tub overnight— finding out exactly what happens when various types get thoroughly watersoaked—to what my husband cheerfully calls "gruesome research." For example, he helped me suspend a suitcase full of books, weighing 98 pounds, in a hall closet. Why? I had to know how far a particular kind of elastic bandage would stretch, over different intervals of time, if it were used to hang a 98-pound woman in the mystery I was then writing. By measuring the elastic bandage suspending the suitcase at different intervals during a 24-hour period, I found out the answer.

Now we come to the third way of getting your information —asking people who *do* know. There are two distinct ways of doing this. The first (and a frequent) method is a casual, innocent-sounding chat, not saying you're a mystery writer and want these facts for a book—just seeming interested and asking questions. That's definitely advisable if you otherwise will run the risk of making people self-conscious or uncommunicative. An example of that was my research at the Washington Square Outdoor Art Show. I was literally underfoot so much, I had to let some of those 125 artists think I was interested in buying their paintings. (It didn't hurt them, and the book gave publicity to the show!)

The second method is stating frankly who you are, and why you're asking. If you do that, will experts in their field give you the information? They may, quite possibly—if your approach is right. But what does that mean?

Well, first, do your own spadework. Don't take an expert's time by asking elementary things you can find out yourself with reasonable research. Unless the expert is a personal friend and really eager to help, never ask him any but those few technical questions you *can't* find out yourself. Remember that the absolute *must*, if he or she gives you an interview, is to say you'll be brief, have your questions written out in advance; and then to *be* brief! This is a cardinal rule, most particularly if you're asking about medical, legal, police or newspaper procedure; but it also applies to plenty of other professions where a busy specialist is kind enough to give you advice. (The minimum courtesy, in return, is to send him a copy of the book when published.)

Incidentally, it's a good idea not to take for granted that you know how public services and utilities operate, just because you're accustomed to using them. If you're concerned with bus schedules and how they vary, don't guess, if you want to make sense. Call the bus company and find out!

And now we come to the finished manuscript of your book. Since my own protagonist is a young woman lawyer, Marka de Lancey, I always—after all the research—ask a lawyer friend to read the entire book before it goes to the publisher. Similarly, if your own main character is a professor of higher mathematics, a motion picture producer, or whatever, I hope you may also have a friend in that field who will read the manuscript for you. It certainly helps in spotting errors, where technical questions are involved. An editor in a publishing house is generally acute in this regard, but he can hardly be an encyclopedia of all trades and professions. The burden of accuracy is on you, the author.

A final suggestion: suppose you are fortunate, let's say, in getting a chance to check on certain medical details with an expert in homicide cases, before you start your book. When you finish it, you understandably do *not* want to bother him a second time. But this you can do—detach from the manuscript those few pages dealing with the actual medical scenes, and ask your own doctor to read them. (Doctors love mystery novels as a rule, and with just a few pages to glance over, your doctor probably won't mind!)

Why ask him to do this? Chiefly for language. (You may, despite careful notes, have misused a medical phrase.) And especially for dialogue. If you think about it, and listen with your inner ear, you'll realize that a doctor has several different kinds of phraseology, gradations of speech. He talks one way to a patient, or to the average layman; quite a different way when he's talking to the police with whom he works on a criminal investigation; and still another way when he's talking with a medical colleague, when he can really talk shop as doctors do among themselves. This same thing applies, in greater or less degree, to engineers, musicians, artists, lawyers, physicists—any technical profession, really, that you can name.

I'd like to close with a word of caution, which I try never to forget myself. Make it authentic—by all means. But not so authentic that you clearly label what you must not label. Don't forget about libel! Fiction writers must not name their characters after real people they know, or have heard of. By the same token, be careful about actual locations and house numbers. Any landlord will be pleased to read about what a pleasant neighborhood and a fine sunny location is 33 Mishtawhickin Avenue. Not so, however, if your murder victim drips blood all the way up to the third-floor landing of Number 33 before the fatal collapse.

In short, with names, actual locations and house numbers, play it safe. What you're after *here*, dear fellow writers of mysteries, is Verisimilitude—*not* Authenticity.

The worst thing that can happen to you is to have someone pick up your story or your book, glance at the first sentence or so, and say, "So what?" And go no further. And never reach the heart of that wonderful story that took you so much time and sweat to produce.

Great books may or may not have great beginnings, but several linger in my mind. "It was the best of times, it was the worst of times ...." *(A Tale of Two Cities)* "Call me Ishmael." *(Moby Dick)* "The bishop was feeling rather seasick." *(South Wind)*

No tricks here. None of the three books I've cited are mysteries, none of those three sentences startles you with a desperate or dramatic situation, and yet each somehow lures you on. Why?

Michael Avallone, who has written several hundred books and is due to write several hundred more, and whose credo is that a professional writer can write anything, knows a good deal about the narrative hook, or, how to make you keep on reading. Note, for instance, that even here, in the first sentence of his chapter, he captures you. But let him go on from there.

13. The Narrative Hook

by Michael Avallone

In 1842, there *was* nothing new under the sun.

That moody genius, Edgar Allan Poe, goosequilling a review of Nathaniel Hawthorne's *Twice-told Tales* for *Graham's Magazine,* had this to say about the art of writing the short story:

"... a skillful literary artist has constructed a tale. If wise, he has not fashioned his thoughts to accommodate his incidents: but having conceived, with deliberate care, a certain unique or single *effect* to be brought out, he then invents such incidents – he then combines such events as may best aid him in establishing this preconceived effect. *If his very initial sentence tends not to the outbringing of this effect, then he has failed in his first step. ..."*

A trifle long-winded, perhaps, but these are Words of Wisdom from the Master, who fathered the American Detective Story in 1841 with "The Murders in the Rue Morgue." Is there a better definition of the *narrative hook* even in this day and age? No, there is not, and any sampling of the very best in all forms of literature will show clearly that Poe's principle is not only peerless but still true.

The haunted titan of Providence certainly played by his own rules, too, as any of his world-famous tales will certify.

"The 'Red Death' had long devastated the country."

Or —

"True! — nervous — very, very dreadfully nervous I had been and am: but why *will* you say that I am mad?"

Or —

"The thousand injuries of Fortunato I had borne as best I could; but when he ventured upon insult, I vowed revenge."

Or —

"I was sick — sick unto death with that long agony; and when they at length unbound me, and I was permitted to sit, I felt that my senses were leaving me."

And last, but definitely not least —

"During the whole of a dull, dark, and soundless day in the autumn of the year, when the clouds hung oppressively low in the heavens, I had been passing alone, on horseback, through a singularly dreary tract of country, and at length found myself, as the shades of the evening drew on, within view of the melancholy House of Usher . . . ."

Any writer or reader worth his salt will easily recognize the dark and direful opening lines of "The Masque of the Red Death," "The Tell-Tale Heart," "The Cask of Amontillado," "The Pit and the Pendulum," and "The Fall of the House of Usher," Grade A specimens of Poe's credo about not wasting a single sentence before establishing the intended effect and mood of the story about to unfold.

Yes, the Master Poe knew what he was talking about. But what about the rest of us? Go to your bookshelf, select any book at random (anthologies of short stories or novels), and you'll probably find that the good books and certainly the great ones, mesh with Poe's ground rule about narrative hooks.

Since this is my article, I'll speak for myself and present a few of my own narrative hooks.

"I'll begin by telling you she was the tallest girl that ever walked into my office."

And, "Conroy was missing."

And, "I hadn't seen Kyle Crosby since the day we blew up the south wall of the SS barracks outside Munich."

Two of these immediately establish the first person as narrator, and all the characters mentioned are *main* characters that sound the keynotes of each particular book. Dolores Ainseley's height is paramount to the puzzle of *The Tall Dolores,* Conroy is a missing nuclear scientist whose disappearance is at the center of *The Living Bomb,* and Kyle Crosby's return from the dead opens the door to the story of *The February Doll Murders.*

So, what all of these hooks, Poe's and mine, have in common, is that they either name, or speak in the person of, a main character. Mine indicate something that will be significant in the plot, and Poe's manage to demonstrate some psychological quirk of the main character. If you're using a first person narrator, you can start showing the way his mind works immediately, but if you're not, go for a plot trick, like Dolores' height. By not identifying Conroy in the first sentence, I create a temporary aura of mysterious significance about him that makes the reader begin to wonder what's up. The mention of the last time "I" saw Kyle Crosby tells the reader that the relationship goes back a long time, makes him wonder why it got interrupted, and tells him that both Crosby and "I" have been in dangerous places doing even more dangerous things.

In short, don't be afraid to get into the middle of plot or character in the first sentence. Poe wasn't, I'm not, and it will pay you not to be.

Over and over again in these pages, in answers to question-naires, in asides in the course of some chapters, in assumptions considered too obvious to bother stating, comes the advice that the creation of character is at the bottom of all good fiction. Know your characters, make them real, familiarize yourself with their backgrounds. Surely, but how?

In this chapter deservedly reprinted, John D. MacDonald, master storyteller, goes into the mechanics of the process and shows how he creates character.

14. How a Character Becomes Believable

by John D. MacDonald

It is, of course, entirely possible to write a successful mystery wherein the characters are merely symbols—two-dimensional personifications of virtues and vices to be moved about within a puzzle plot until by the final page they fit the pattern of solution as neatly as the flat pieces of a completed jigsaw puzzle. But today this sort of mystery is the exception rather than the rule—as it was a few years ago. Raymond Chandler's classic article in the Atlantic, "The Gentle Art of Murder," covers this shift of emphasis thoroughly and definitively.

Today a less patient public requires more suspense than mystification, more action than cerebration. Purists will not recognize the novel of action and suspense as a mystery. Indeed, they will be content with flatness of character, so long as there is a carefully interwoven web of clue and counterclue. Unfortunately the purists do not form a sufficiently large market.

That leads us directly to my point. There is nothing more dreadful than the "mystery" novel of action and suspense wherein the characters have that peculiar woodenness characteristic of the English school of the mystery story, genus 1925. We can see, therefore, that as the mystery story becomes less dependent on intricacy of plot and detection, it becomes ever more dependent on the depicting of characters "in the round." And as the characters in mystery fiction become ever more fully realized, the dividing line between the mystery and the straight novel becomes constantly more vague (*e.g.*, the work of Margaret Millar).

Thus, insofar as lead protagonists are concerned, the rules of depicting character—if indeed we can affirm that any rules exist—differ in no significant way as between the straight novel and the mystery.

I shall now talk about these "rules" for the lead characters, with the warning that they are the result of my own thinking about my own work, and should be carefully examined before you make any assumption that they can be applicable to your work.

1. The first-person treatment is seriously self-limiting. The "I" must say all that is in his mind and heart. There is no good way to dimensionalize that "I." All psychic reactions are flattened out. With good cause, it is rarely attempted in the serious novel. Saul Bellow attempted it in 1953. Because he is basically a craftsman, he sustains his lead character throughout the action, but then he, too, succumbs to a curious fate, which seems typical of most of the "I" characters in fiction, particularly mystery fiction.

The character can be sustained for the length of the book, but soon the outline of the man begins to blur. Philip Marlowe, Mike Hammer—regardless of merit in the handling, cleverness in treatment, they all blend into one faceless, characterless, depersonalized "I" remembered vaguely for only those common qualities of durability and determination. Think back to those better books written in the first person, and see how much more clearly you remember the secondary leads, those people who had the character-building advantage of third-person handling.

Yet we continue to do first-person mysteries because it is a device which simplifies the problem of reader participation in the action. We accept the self-limitation and do everything we can to sustain the lead through the book, perfectly aware that the lead will sink back into anonymity as soon as the book is closed.

I am about half through the first draft of a first-person mystery as yet untitled. Here is a part where I try to give the lead character some dimension, something a bit beyond his being a walking, talking tape recorder.

> I stood and waited. It was a long afternoon. I moved with the shade. The long gray of the Spanish moss hung from the oaks in the windless stillness. Chickens scratched at the baked yards of the cabins, and made the throaty sounds of heat, blurred and querulous. One of the women came out and slapped the soapy gray phlegm of dishwater into the yard and stood for a moment with the pan in her hand, looking toward me, *telling me that I was out of time and place.* She went back in and the door spring made a thin musical note before it slapped the screen back into place. *I stood in an alien place, out of focus to myself, as though I had lost some part of my own identity and meaning. And I thought of other places and other times of waiting.* The afternoon was long. And very hot.

I have taken the liberty of italicizing those portions of the above passage which I hope give the observer more depth. He stands there, on the edge of self-doubt, believing in what he is doing only through habit rather than conviction.

Yet is not the woman much more vivid, without anything having been said about her?

The old saw about "Don't tell 'em, show 'em" cannot be considered applicable to the character of the first person. You have to tell 'em, but tell 'em as indirectly as possible, achieving your effect through a feeling of mood rather than being too explicit.

Not "I stood in an alien place wondering how I had gotten

into this business, and I thought that as soon as this case was over I would try to make the break again. Then I remembered that I had told myself that same thing a lot of times in the past. And yet here I was."

And the devil of it is, you have to hook that very indirectness which is almost your only way of achieving any dimensionalism of character up to a scene or situation which furthers the story line. In the example I used, the reader is perfectly aware that the quiet, hot afternoon is going to end in a violence peculiarly fitted to the scene. And thus, having built to a point of suspense, I can back off safely, just enough, to try to make my lead guy "rounder." The straight novel gives more leeway. It permits incidents designed solely to depict character more fully. We must wrench at our incidents which further plot until we have them in a form that will enable us to round out character without slowing action.

But, to repeat myself, the first-person viewpoint is sadly self-limiting as far as the character development of the lead is concerned. It requires the most careful handling, and offers the least reward.

2. The third-person handling of character is the simplest. It is applicable, of course, to the secondary leads in the first-person mystery and to all the leads in the third-person treatment. Here the "show 'em" rule comes thoroughly into its own.

Here is another excerpt from the same work in progress:

The music had been quiet and pleasant, but the program changed to a newscaster who was neither. She made a face at me and got up with that air of dramatic slowness and crossed to the small radio and clicked it off. The room was very still. She stood with her back to me and took a final puff at her cigarette and, as she turned slowly, she attempted to stub it out in a glass ash tray beside the small radio. But she missed the ash tray and, sensing what she had done, she turned back with the first hasty movement I had seen her make. She made a sharp hissing intake of breath, brushed the coals to the floor, licked her finger and rubbed hard at the blistered varnish, continuing the futile scrubbing until long after any need for it was over. When she turned again to face me I saw that we were through fencing.

The above is more satisfying to me—and I hope to the reader—than to say, "I knew that all her calmness and slow easy movements were fake. I could see she was nervous but concealing it. I knew that if I waited long enough, she'd break. It might be some little thing that would do it. Some flaw in her poise. And when she stubbed out her cigarette on the table top, missing the ash tray completely, I knew I had her rattled, and I saw right away she was going to talk."

Both passages give the reader the same information. Thus, if that information is essential to the story line, the story line has not been altered in either case. But in the first passage, there seems to me to be more of the feeling of the woman and her conflict, more empathy. There has been more of a superimposing of character on the bones of plot.

It is in line with the classic example of saying either, "Janice sat up and pulled the pillowcase over her head" or, "Janice was a very shy girl."

3. Regardless of point of view, there is the inevitable problem of avoiding too simplified a character—the villain too villainous, the hero too heroic. I think it is perfectly obvious to any writer that if you attempted to give a complete picture of any human being, one lifetime would not be long enough to do a thorough job. Thus we must be selective. We must stay with meaningful and believable conflict. The man who is utterly certain of himself and his mission is fool, saint or psychopath. Self-doubt might be considered, perhaps, to be the most common denominator of mankind. Thus I am sick unto death of those men and women in mystery fiction whose

only indecision is in whom to shoot first.

Too often in mystery fiction, the attempt to devise a real and believable detective has degenerated into a complication of props rather than expanded into a complication of character, a subtlety and complexity of the spirit. The original fault is perhaps due to that misinterpretation of Sherlock Holmes which places too much weight on the needle, the violin, the pipe. We remember Holmes as a man who, primarily, was troubled in spirit, was obsessed with the sense of evil, whose arrogance was defensive. Yet we see around us today a score of fictional detectives who have been given merely the props without the spirit. They have been given complications involving beer and orchids, jazz and rosebushes, and all manner of physical distortions, twitches, spasms and odd habits. It is as though the author sat down and deliberately fabricated the most incredible detective he could imagine—with the childlike faith that through eccentricities he could define character.

Here we can learn from another field. Compare one of these bizarre creations with Sergeant Joe Friday. Even within the intellectual limitations of the mystery over radio and TV, we find that somehow we have come to know Friday as a man. A man, not a prefabricated device.

I cannot try to illustrate this third point through any specific passage from work in progress. I hope that the whole book will make the reader feel, when he sets it down, that he has met a man; that I have not tricked him. I hope to make him a man by getting into the book enough of the characteristics of a man—the glories and the stinks, the shame and the pride, the doubt and the angers, the deceits and the pity. I must be aware that I am writing a mystery story but at no time when I am touching on those incidents that help build character can I have my tongue anywhere near my cheek. Those parts I must do as well and with as much sincerity as I can. Because I know that it is the fully realized characters in my lead spots that are going to hoist the book successfully over the hurdles of plot inconsistencies, of too much use of coincidence.

Also, in another way, those lead characters are going to keep me out of trouble. If they become human and believable by page 50, they will permit me to do nothing inconsistent with them by page 100. They seem to assist in the action and even to suggest action. That is why I can never work to outline. I know where the end will be. I know the beginning. And once I have men and women in the story, they will help guide it through the middle areas of the story.

Now, to discuss minor characters in mystery fiction—the walk-on parts. Under normal conditions the mystery writer is called on to handle successfully more minor characters than the straight novelist. And he must handle them in a way that will leave the sharpest possible impact on the reader.

To go back to that first example I quoted. One part of it: "One of the women came out and slapped the soapy gray phlegm of dishwater into the yard and stood for a moment with the pan in her hand, looking toward me." That is the only time she appears. She is a part of mood and scene. And she informs the reader that the man waiting is observed and knows he is being observed. I felt that I could more effectively describe her by describing her action. I see her as close to forty, lean, red-knuckled, gray hair, work-worn, cotton dress, faded and sweaty, barefoot and, when she looks toward the man, no expression at all. A sort of blank-faced hostility, yet a hostility too worn down by poverty to be sharp. Something dulled about it.

But if I go into a description that complete, what have I gained if I can give the reader the same general impression, but with more vividness, by describing the action of throwing the dishwater into the yard?

What I am saying is that there must be a very intensified selectivity when you deal with the minor character in mystery fiction. There is where your prose must get as lean and effective as you can make it. Always, of course, understanding the risk of getting too cute—of saying something like, "She had a face like a broken promise and a body like the end of a long winter."

I will go back to a few other passages from the book in progress. This is a salesman on a used-car lot. He figures twice in the action in minor ways. "He was a shy-eyed little man and somebody, or maybe some rule book they have for such places, had convinced him he should be bluff and jovial and hearty as can be, so he kept giving off whoops of laughter as he showed me the stock, and a couple of times he slapped my shoulder or nudged me, but he did it very gingerly as though it was something he didn't like to do, something that offended him a bit but must be controlled, like a ballerina's hangnail."

Notice that the only physically descriptive word in there is "little." Take your choice as to whether he is thin or fat, dark or light, shabby or dapper. You see a specific somebody. And that's enough. That's all I want. And what you see will be more satisfying to you than what I *make* you see by putting in too much physical description.

In another part there is a small girl. "She stood off to the left of the conversation and she had a mouth full of those braces that come equipped with rubber bands. She kept boinging one of the rubber bands with the tip of her tongue, playing a small grave counterpoint to all our grown-up talk." That is all there is about her. But it is essential to a part of the action to know that one of the principals does have a girl child. This seemed, to me, to be a happier way of getting the information across.

Now, because all of these things are inextricably mingled, I want to say something that took me a hell of a lot longer to learn than it reasonably should have. I only hope I can say it clearly. Take these three examples of minor characters.

Okay, in each case the character is being observed and described by my lead character. The selectivity of his observation, the things he sees and points out through selection, are continual character clues to the lead character himself. Thus, before you touch the shorthand description of any minor character, you must first pause and select *not* what you would see, but what *he* would see, based on his background, his environment, the sort of person he is. My stories were falling apart in some obscure way because I was not consistent in my viewpoint. I would be looking through the eyes of my first-person or third-person lead, and then describe what I, myself, would see, and the effect was to flatten everything out. Maintaining viewpoint in external description is, to me, one of the most difficult parts of the whole thing. And yet it is the most satisfying when you do it well, because you have gently informed your reader of more aspects of the character of your lead without it being obvious that you are doing so.

To underline my point, perhaps unnecessarily, I will do that small girl again from the viewpoint of someone else in the conversation and note that the description is consistently external. "She stood off to the left and she wore one of those braces that have a rubber band stretched tautly across the back of it. She kept thrumming the rubber band with her tongue, changing the shape of her mouth to produce different tones, waiting vacantly for the conversation to end."

Now, even though the changes are slight, can you not detect a difference in the attitude toward children of the first observer and the second observer? One example may indeed show a slight difference only. But if consistency is maintained throughout the book, the difference is great, and not only sharpens the minor characters but deepens the lead character.

Hemingway is the great master of this phase of technique. His objectivity is the most subtle and delicate subjectivity imaginable. When Spanish prisoners walk up a road, he describes the road and the weather. But so selective is his external description that you learn, merely through selection, the sort of men the prisoners are, and their current mood. It is never the road or the weather that Hemingway sees. He is not there. He does not permit himself to be there. His discipline is flawless. And of course, I must say regretfully, the result of an awful lot of brute labor—more than most of us are willing to contribute.

Effective delineation of character was once, in mystery fiction, the frosting on the cake. Now, I am afraid, it has become the cake itself, with plot intricacies the frosting. It requires, and justly I believe, the greatest amount of work, and yields the greatest rewards. It is, after all, the art of writing about people rather than things.

Janet Gregory Vermandel turned from writing advertising copy to writing suspense novels. In the course of her work she has been particularly interested in the problems of point of view. John D. MacDonald discussed some of the differences between first and third person point of view, but there's a lot more to it than that, as she so ably points out.

15. Deciding on Viewpoint

by Janet Gregory Vermandel

Some writers know instinctively which viewpoint is the best one for the story they are about to tell. For them, it isn't a question of first person or third person but rather how to use a character's viewpoint to strengthen and individualize that character, as John D. MacDonald illustrates so clearly in the preceding chapter. Other writers, and I am among them, have to wrestle first with the problem of who is going to tell the story. Not how to use viewpoint most effectively, but *which viewpoint to use*.

I once paid a literary agent, the kind who charges budding authors a reading fee, fifty dollars to read my first book manuscript (written from multiple viewpoint) and tell me where I had gone wrong. It was money well spent. His advice was simple. "Decide who your main character is. Don't let there be any doubt about it. Tell your story from his/her point of view. Stick with one point of view."

It was sound advice for a beginning writer. I took it and wrote my next four suspense novels in the first person. After the first book, writing in the first person wasn't an artistic decision; it was the result of limited confidence. I understood first person viewpoint but I wasn't very sure about any other. I wasted a lot of time in indecision and false starts before I finally settled on third person viewpoint for the fifth book and multiple viewpoint for the one after that.

Sometimes the story itself dictates which point of view you should use, but sometimes it doesn't, and it helps to have a clear idea of what choices you have and the merits of each.

There are two major points of view from which a story can be told — omniscient and character. Within the character category come first person and third person (major character), viewpoint, multiple viewpoint, and narrator-observer (minor character) viewpoint. Not all of them work for all stories and the one you select affects the flavor and impact of your story, as well as the plot.

Omniscient viewpoint offers the most freedom. It permits you, as author, to see, know, and explore everything that serves the story line. You tell your story from the outside, commenting on anything you choose, from the weather to existentialism. You may do it impersonally, as the all-knowing, godlike author, without crediting the comment to any particular character within the story, *e.g.,* "It was another bright, windswept day," or you can move freely through the minds of your characters, *e.g.,* "Jane remembered the last time they had talked of Dugal. It had taken days for the hurtful memories to subside again. Watching her eyes change, Alan realized that Jane still lived with that tragedy."

The omniscient point of view is ideal for the journalistic, heavily researched book. The all-knowingness of the author can create reader belief by feeding in substantial amounts of convincing corroborative detail that would be difficult to include if it had to be funneled through one or several characters' firsthand knowledge, as witness *Day of the Jackal.*

There is another possible benefit. Suppose your natural writing style is a particularly literary one suitable to, say, the writing of essays, but you prefer to write modern suspense novels. You must create (by ruthless pruning and tightening) believable contemporary characters in a contemporary setting. If you use first or third person point of view, that pretty well takes care of your entire story, but it strains your natural style. Suppose, however, that you use omniscient viewpoint. Although your dialogue and characters' observations still must be contemporary in flavor, the narrative style of the rest of the story can follow your natural bent, so long as you don't slow down the action. And your book may well be more interesting because of the contrast in textures. Critics are occasionally impressed by writers who employ this technique with sufficient panache.

Character viewpoint lets you tell your story through the eyes of one or more characters within the story, knowing and revealing only what the character knows and feels.

First person or *third person* viewpoint (of a major character) has the advantage of telling the story from one point of view, usually the hero's or heroine's. This seems to me the most direct way of getting the story down on paper and controlling the elements that good suspense fiction demands. However, both first and third person viewpoints make plotting more difficult. Your viewpoint character, whether "I," "he," or "she," has to be on the scene at all times in order to tell the story, but you cannot afford to have him or your readers know everything that is happening or you sacrifice suspense. Resolving that plot dilemma takes ingenuity but authors do it successfully all the time.

Multiple viewpoint makes plotting easier but story structure more complicated. It involves telling the story from the point of view of several characters in turn, by chapters (which can make for a jumpy book if done to excess) or by sections, whichever better serves your plot. If you tell your story from the point of view of three or four characters, you usually treat all of them in the same manner, *i.e.* all in first person or all in third person, but give one character prominence over the others, according to his role in the story and your own skill.

Notable advantages of using multiple viewpoint are, (1) it's easy to show your readers what everyone is up to, on stage so to speak, when it suits your purpose. And (2) it's possible to build suspense by leaving one character cliff-hanging at chapter's end and skipping to another one's exploits in the following chapter. However, this technique demands a nice sense of balance. Too obvious and too frequent skipping about will turn off, rather than titillate, a reader's appetite for suspense. Also, with several viewpoint characters sharing the limelight, you have to concentrate on tightness and pacing to prevent your story from losing focus.

Narrator-observer viewpoint is that of a minor character in the story, as in Somerset Maugham's short stories and the Sherlock Holmes adventures recounted by Dr. Watson. Although technically a minor character, the narrator is basically outside the story action. He is interested, often partisan, but always on the fringes of the action. He never influences events. His role is that of observer, someone with whom the reader can identify, who knows only what he sees or is told when it suits the story's purpose. He may have specialized knowledge of his own (as doctor, lawyer, family friend), which makes him convincing as an observer, but is often mystified by the events of the story or mistaken in his conclusions, both of which can help you in misdirecting the reader and achieving a strong surprise ending.

I believe that every writer has one natural viewpoint which comes to him most easily and switches to others as befits his plot or inclination. My own, much as I wish it otherwise, is first person and any book I write gets written more easily when I stick to it. But that may be merely familiarity. It is also my opinion that it pays to try them all, if possible. In this business you never know where your advantage lies.

A technical problem specific to the mystery story is whether or not to use a Watson. Rex Stout's article, reprinted from the previous edition, explores the possibilities. Fortunately for all mystery fans, Stout decided on a Nero Wolfe and an Archie Goodwin.

16. What to Do About a Watson

by Rex Stout

As Poe invented not only the skeleton of the detective story but also its organs and most of its muscles, there is a temptation to add that he invented Watson too as a device peculiarly useful for the genre; but he didn't. First-person narration of his tales had become a settled habit with Poe before he ever created Dupin, and to Dupin's Boswell he gave no name at all but "I." Conan Doyle, in acknowledging his debt to Poe, did not say whether he adopted the "I" deliberately as the best solution for certain technical problems, so Watson himself, at birth, may have been merely incidental. Possibly, like Topsy, he jest growed.

Whether a fictional detective should have a Watson can be profitably discussed only as a technical problem. A Watson may of course be developed into a colorful and interesting character in his own right, but so can any other member of the cast, even the victim or the culprit. The question is, other things being equal, are you more likely to write a good detective story with a Watson than without one?

I think you are. (I speak, of course, of a detective story, not a sex-and-gin marathon or a cloak-and-dagger *geste* or a "novel of suspense.") A Watson can be a devil of a nuisance at times, but he is worth it for his wonderful cooperation in clearing the toughest hurdle on the course.

For if you are sticking to the true detective story, not joining the army of modern hybridizers who are bent on giving it so new a look that not even Sherlock Holmes would suspect its ancestry, your main technical difficulty will be the same as Wilkie Collins' and Conan Doyle's. The hour comes when you have your cast and the frame of your plot, and enough of the clues and convolutions to start with. From there on you share with all other storytellers, dead and alive, great and small, the responsibility of making your pages readable, your people interesting and your events notable. But you have a special responsibility. The detective is your hero, and the central and most significant events must be the steps that lead him to his triumph. Not only that, you must somehow manage to show or plainly indicate the steps without letting the reader grasp their full significance.

That's where a Watson is a jewel and a blessing. It can be done without him, but not so gracefully or naturally. Say your detective hero, Lord Peter Poirot, on page 94, has to make a phone call. You must let the reader know the call is made, for on page 229 it will cover an essential point in the elucidation; but you dare not let the reader hear what was said because he would then know too much.

If you say that is cheating the reader you are quite right, but you are ruled out of order. That kind of cheat has been indulged in over and over by every fictional detective, without exception, from Sherlock Holmes to Perry Mason. The point is, how best to get away with it? If your detective is himself telling the story the cheat is so flagrant that the reader will quit on you. If you, the author, are telling it in the third person, it is less flagrant, but still obvious and offensive, and the reader will swallow it with difficulty no matter how ingeniously you cover it. If one of the characters is telling it, especially one of the suspects, no question of cheating is involved, but you have another problem equally difficult, how to keep the "I" from becoming the hero (or, more usually, heroine), with your detective relegated to the background. If that happens you may come up with a good story, but not, properly speaking, a detective story. In a true detective story the detective is it. But if a Watson tells it? Then it's a cinch. Like this:

"Evidently," said I, "Mr. Wilson's assistant counts for a good deal in this mystery of the Red-headed League. I am sure that you inquired your way merely in order that you might see him."

"Not him."

"What then?"

"The knees of his trousers."

"And what did you see?"

"What I expected to see."

"Why did you beat the pavement?"

"My dear doctor, this is a time for observation, not for talk."

That's the way to do it!

Richard Martin Stern has written short-shorts, short stories, novelettes, mystery novels, and full-length, ten-dollar novels. All of them have held interest at least partly because he is a superb technician; he knows what suspense is and how to create it. He discusses suspense in the following article, and note that he, too, emphasizes the importance of character.

17. Suspense

by Richard Martin Stern

What is there to say about suspense in fiction? That it belongs in whodunits and cliff-hanging adventure tales, and has no place in straight, serious fiction? Poppycock.

Suspense in its broadest form is the stuff of which all fiction is, or ought to be, made. It is suspense that catches the reader's interest, carries him along with you, makes him turn the page and read on instead of putting the book down for, maybe, another time. Think about it. Would you go back into the theatre for the last act of, say, *Hamlet,* if the author had not led you with conscious craft to the point where you simply had to know what was going to happen and how? Isn't that what suspense is all about?

Or take what I have read, that people lined the wharf in New York waiting for the mail packet from England to dock so they could read the latest installment of Dickens's *Old Curiosity Shop* and relieve their anxiety about whether Little Nell had indeed died. If that is not suspense, I don't know the meaning of the word.

But how does the beginning writer manage to achieve it?

Ah, there we get to the heart of the matter, and I do not pretend that I have any formula for instant success, but there are certain guidelines that can be set forth.

First and foremost, the reader must care. That is one of those remarks so obvious that too many writers forget it. The reader must care, and that means that he must have an interest in the characters. Plot, alone, will not do it. People are born, fall in love, grow sick and die every day, but you don't know them and so what happens to them is not really important to you. But when these events happen to someone close, someone you care about, then they become the stuff of drama and you await their outcome in a mood that can only be called suspenseful.

How many stories or books have you and I started to read and then tossed aside because we didn't give a damn what happened to the names that appeared on the pages? All manner of weird and wonderful things could be going on, but unless the writer had given us characters with whom we could identify and about whom we could care, we lost the urge to turn the page; there was no quality of suspense.

In remarks he made at West Point, William Faulkner kept returning to a single phrase: 'the human heart in conflict.' Or, as my agent used to ask too often about my stories, "Where is the love versus duty?" A phrase and a question that go directly to character, which is where it all begins.

That is not to say that plot is unimportant in the building of suspense. Plot is very important, obviously, because without it nothing happens and, as in what I call 'navel novels', in which everybody sits around cross-legged contemplating his identity crisis, what is suspenseful about that?

And so characters there must be about whom the reader cares, and plot to provide action and demonstrate the human heart in conflict — quite probably about love versus duty. Now you have the tools with which to build suspense. How do you go about it?

Well, one way you do *not* go about it is by trickery. Dishonesty will out and become in the current jargon 'counterproductive.' A writer friend of mine observes that if your character opens a can of beans, somebody has to eat them. And Chekhov insisted that, if, in the first chapter a gun hangs on the wall, in an early following chapter without fail, that

gun has to be fired. You can do all manner of things to misdi-
rect your reader, as a magician on-stage misdirects your attention, but the rabbit you eventually pull out of the hat has
to be a real rabbit, not a mouse you sneaked in at the last
moment as a substitute. Level with your reader and he will
go along; cheat him and you have lost your audience. So
much for the don'ts.

On the positive side, there are two words I keep always
in mind. They are *intention* and *anticipation,* and while they
are not the same, in fact are quite dissimilar, together they
can open the door for suspense. The *intention* is the character's, and it must come first, because its function is to produce
anticipation in the reader's mind; which in turn gives rise
to the suspense we are aiming at. Hamlet declares his intention to catch the conscience of the king. You care about Hamlet, and so immediately, out of your own knowledge and experience, you begin to anticipate some of the problems he is
going to face, to estimate the odds against him; and inevitably, if unconsciously, you wonder if he can possibly succeed,
and if so, how? Or will he fail? You hunch forward a little
in your seat while you wait to find out, and isn't that precisely
what Shakespeare was trying to accomplish?

There are, of course, other ways to produce antici-
pation-suspense. There is, for example, a dam at the head
of the valley. Torrential rains have flooded the valley itself,
and while the major problems of the story concentrate on
the efforts of the people in the valley to save what they can
of their livestock and their personal belongings from the
flood, the reader is already keeping one eye on that dam.
If it bursts, everything is suddenly and dramatically changed.
Is this not the stuff of which suspense is made?

Time, is, of course, a powerful tool for the building of
suspense. The minutes, the hours are ticking away, and will
whatever is going to happen take place in time? Will John
Wayne reach the pass before the rascals have gone through?

Turn the pages and see. In a recent novel of mine called *The Tower,* the entire action takes place in less than twelve hours, and the major action in a little over four. For purposes of plot (suspense) it was mandatory that the ticking minutes be emphasized. I used the simple device, by no means original, of heading each chapter with its time span, thereby making time itself a part of the story. Thus: 9:00 a.m. - 9:33 a.m.; 11:10 a.m. - 12:14 p.m.; etc. The final paragraph reads, "The time was 8:41. It had been four hours and eighteen minutes since the explosion." I have been told that the device was successful.

Sequence is another important factor in the building of suspense. Again, it ought to be obvious, but I am afraid it isn't always. How many books or stories have you and I read in which the writer has shot the works, halfway through his tale, and from that point on has to plod downhill? Where then has suspense gone?

Sometimes I like to think of a story as a kind of hill climb. You start at the bottom and work your way up. There are dips and rises, but always you are working toward the top of the hill. When you arrive at the top, which is the story's climax, you face a steep drop-off, and you get to the bottom just as quickly as you can. Why? Because you have used up your suspense, you have shot the works, you have sung your big aria and, to continue to mix the figures of speech, you want to get off-stage while the audience is still applauding.

A writer friend of mine once asked, "Where do you go when you've started your story on High C?" Good question, and I think the answer is that you drop an octave or two as fast as you can and then start climbing again. You want your story to build, its pace to quicken, its excitement to grow — then you are building the suspense and pulling the reader along with you.

In the heyday of the great national magazines, the "slicks," the craft of serial writing reached a high state of expertise. Basically, the serial was a single story running through, let us say, three installments of thirty pages each. (There could be as few as two installments, or as many as eight, but the technical problems remained the same.) Each installment had to carry on the main story, but it also had to have a smaller story of its own, a sub-plot, if you will, or at least a large problem presented but not completely solved, thereby whetting the reader's appetite for the next issue, in which problem number one would be solved, and problem number two presented. And so on, the main story rising in pitch to the final installment in which everything was solved and the story quickly ended.

It is, I think, not a bad format to keep in mind. Probably because I served my apprenticeship in the slicks, I find it ingrained in my subconscious. Always the tension must rise, but never too fast. Like a pot that must not be allowed to boil over, there are times when you must reduce the heat, slow down, let the reader take a few easy breaths and maybe go out to the refrigerator for a fresh beer. Then start at him again, making your story rise, quicken, making the tension mount. This is the essence, and whether you are writing mystery, adventure, romance, or 'serious' fiction, whether you're writing for juveniles or adults, for hardcover or soft, this is the art of making the reader turn the page. This is suspense.

Dorothy Salisbury Davis' novels are rich with her own peculiar style and mood, and she is particularly able to tell us about background and atmosphere. Note how rich and even spine-chilling are the examples that slide so easily off her pen — or, to be more precise, which click off her typewriter. She is a master of this kind of effect.

18. Background and Atmosphere

by Dorothy Salisbury Davis

No doubt some writers are good talkers, but, to my mind, good writers are necessarily even better listeners. They are receptive not merely to the ideas which sputter out of talk, but to the sputtering itself, the instinctive selection of words, images, illustrations plucked out of the environment in which the talk occurs, be it the corner bar, the intensive care unit of a hospital, a logging camp, or a police lock-up. They are receptive, too, to the ambience of place, its felicitousness, its hostility — its vibrations, if you will. The writer absorbs background as naturally as he breathes air. It becomes the reservoir from which his work continually draws its vitality.

Very often the idea for a story comes out of background, a setting which gets to a writer. What a place for a murder! Which of us has not said that? But wherever the idea comes from, it is imperative that it *seem* to come out of its background, that the crime could only have happened where it did.

Background, in the structural sense, is where the action occurs. It is the scene in which diverse characters are interrupted in their normal pursuits by the occurrence of something abnormal. A sentence like "A stranger came to our village," can set off a reader's imagination without a descriptive adjective because the word "village" suggests a small community of people who know one another and the word "stranger" suggests a new, disruptive element. The contrast creates almost instant suspense. But for the suspense to hold, the background must become as solid as the action is fluid. We must know the people, their houses, church, clubs, traditions — in a word, the lore of the place. Background is the credible scene which makes the incredible event, when it happens, the more deliciously bizarre and, paradoxically, the more believable. The ring of authenticity in background establishes faith between reader and writer.

It may seem that I am suggesting long swatches of descriptive prose. I'm not. Adjectives, by and large, are dead words. Like it or not, we are living in the age of the verb. It is imperative to the modern mystery that background and action be strongly integrated. And this, I suggest, is best accomplished by the lively use of character.

Background is actually composed of two elements, place and people. The people—secondary characters, in craft parlance — integrate place and plot; they must, then, be a part of the action. In the mystery story, they function as witnesses. Character is dealt with elsewhere in this book, so I shall concern myself here only with its function in projecting background, but it is an arbitrary line which must not be drawn in practice.

Select people with personal color as well as vital functions in the community. By community I mean village, city, laboratory, university, international compound, whatever. Try to give their speech freshness by creating allusions which sound like the language of their trades or their mother-lore. I have a personal antipathy toward written dialect. It is obstructive to the reader, and since it is basically an unfamiliar sound given to an otherwise familiar word, the spelling of the sound is open to any number of choices. The pattern of speech and the choice of images quite adequately convey the character's origins. ("He's the beggar at the pump with his cup running

over, but he can't see the water for the tears in his eyes."
What would I have added to that characterization by spelling
water, *watther* or *wather* or *waather*?)

The use of foreign words or phrases to bolster a sense
of locale is more generally felicitous. I have used them myself,
combining them with the rest of the speech in English, but
I think they are a crutch that sticks out.

I know of no other way to achieve verisimilitude of place
than, to the extent of one's ability, to become a part of that
place oneself. It involves that particular kind of listening I
spoke of in the beginning. It involves seeing, touching, smell-
ing, tasting. But since words are the mode of our com-
munication, listening is our prime obligation to ourselves as
writers.

Curiosity never killed a mystery writer. Poke in dark
corners, explore abandoned structures. I don't mean merely
the structures of buildings, but of businesses, and dreams;
look into the sites and circumstances of sealed up cyclotrons,
coal mines, theaters, churches where nobody prays any more.
In every defeated dream there is a story, and one susceptible
of violence, and the place where it began is the background.
Don't be afraid to ask questions. Wait for the answers; and
oh, dear writer, have the patience to understand the answers.
Think of Sherlock Holmes and his pipe.

A veteran mystery writer used to say you could get away
with a smattering of background knowledge by making your
protagonist an outsider coming on that particular scene for
the first time. This still holds, of course, but not as firmly
as it once did. So much is known in our times about so many
things. Patently, it is not possible to become a physicist in
order to write about murder in a high-energy installation.
But it is both possible and desirable to know a physicist. I
once interviewed a physicist and asked questions that pro-
voked her to thrust a book in my hands. "Before we talk,"
she said, "read this. Any fifteen-year-old could understand

it." Under that challenge I learned more about physics in one night than I could have in a year of self-motivation. An invaluable short-cut to creating believable background is the use of words indigenous to the occupation of the characters. I think of a policeman "taking a squeal." My friend, the physicist, corrected my reference to "the experiment," which, in the trade, is simply referred to as "experiment." A handy writer's gadget is a file box in which to note the patois of various professions, adding to it a colorful phrase or anecdote when one comes your way. File under actor, burglar, cab-driver, doctor, and so on.

Study the motion picture for the effective use of background to suggest atmosphere. What is called the Establishing Shot tells the viewer where he is. Someone making a call from an outdoor phone booth against the interfering noise of traffic, the impatience of others waiting to use the phone, the graffiti on a dirty brick wall, swiftly combine to establish "city." The protagonist's selection of a record on a juke box identifies immediately: an interior scene, the protagonist's taste in music, his concern — or lack of it — for the other patrons, and the reaction of the patrons themselves.

A street vendor always adds color and can add much more. In the mystery he should have at least a small part in the action: he may get in the way of the protagonist, who is in a hurry; the protagonist may upset his wares producing some colorful language; he may button into the protagonist with a vaguely menacing hard sell, and he is always a potential witness. And if you have picked up the patter of his trade, the background is richer, the story stronger, because when he comes in again he will immediately recall that first vivid picture of him.

Any mode of travel in which the writer uses a detail of place that suggests tension — the protagonist's concern for an attaché case among overhead luggage and the people aware of this concern — starts action simultaneously with the showing of background.

The involvement of the protagonist in some "power" operation is good. Excavation machinery comes to mind, high power tools, a police dispatch room. The stronger the link between action and background at the opening, the less necessity for detail in background.

The beginning writer — indeed, the veteran as well — often gets hung up on getting a character into a room, or the scene where the action is to start. Why not start in the room, the action already under way? Then move back from the particular to encompass as much of the general as is needed. Given striking particulars, readers are marvelously adept at filling in background for themselves.

A rule of my own that I try not to violate: have at least a line or two of dialogue on the first page. Its very visibility is a kind of come-on to the reader, telling him that action is imminent, that people are coming into the story at once, and people are the principal ingredient of story.

And every time I sit down to work I say to myself: Show, don't tell. Showing is action, involvement. Telling is preparation for or explanation of action, and should be unnecessary.

If I were to advise you to study one writer for believable and economical background, it would be Georges Simenon.

Atmosphere in the mystery is like *rubato* in music: used judiciously, it heightens the experience; over-used, it blows up into sentimental mush. Atmosphere is distortion for effect. It plays upon the emotions of the characters, and therefore of the reader. The protagonist is particularly susceptible to it. Atmosphere contributes to suspense, roughly, in the way background strengthens action. And here again credibility is crucial. Atmosphere for its own sake is as unacceptable as a character who has no function in the plot.

Once again I am going to film for an example: in that old classic, *The Informer,* Gyppo is looking in a store window. He is cold and the night is wet. He is looking at an advertisement for a Bermuda cruise. The wind picks up flotsam from the street and wraps a paper around his legs. As he peels it off, he sees that it is the "wanted" flyer on Frankie McPhillips, 10 pounds reward. The tapping of the blind singer's cane is the only sound. Here is a perfect orchestration of atmosphere, background, and action.

We must all choose our own images. Contrast is the key: light and shadow, the grotesque which becomes familiar or the familiar which reveals itself to be grotesque: the cloaked figure in the moonlight that turns out to be a tree stump; or the tree stump which suddenly assaults the victim. The sound like machine-gun fire breaking out on a quiet street may turn out to be a cop drawing his nightstick across a window grate. To me, storm is a willow tree flailing in the wind, downed wires hissing with sparks, the blackened chimney of a hurricane lamp; fear is the smell of one's own sweat, a dry tongue. The deeper and more varied the exploitation of the senses, the better. There is a kind of reverse imagery I like: the building flooded with light when not a soul is moving through it; the dark deed in daylight.

It goes without saying that the kind of mystery story you are writing determines the degree and kind of atmosphere you want. So-called straight suspense is generally heavy with atmosphere. I think it is fair to say that books aimed at a woman's audience are richer in atmosphere than others, with the lush, eerie feeling of lurking horror.

There are shortcuts, of course, and fancying myself an economical writer, I particularly like them, the single strokes that set the mood: "I could hear the clack of my heels on the bare floors as I went from room to room to see that nothing was left." The meowing of a cat behind a locked door, the ringing of the telephone at four in the morning.

A very good atmospheric gambit is the dream. Remember in *Wild Strawberries,* the coffin sliding from the carriage and bursting open to reveal that the corpse was the dreamer?

Or, "Last night I dreamt I went to Manderley again." Who would not take that for an opening?

Finally, I go to a poet for the epitome of atmospheric menace. Surely there is no more chilling opening to any fiction, prose or poetry, than Robert Browning's:

"That's my last Duchess painted on the wall,
Looking as if she were alive . . . ."

Stories have been written entirely in dialogue, and with no dialogue whatsoever, but the appearance of at least some dialogue tends to attract readers. Perhaps the best way to check the dialogue you've written is to read it aloud, so that the false and the stilted and the unnatural jar your ears. But how do you write it in the first place?

Two articles, by Margery Allingham and Carl G. Hodges, reprinted from the earlier edition, discuss the problem and give some helpful examples.

19. Dialogue

by Margery Allingham and Carl G. Hodges

First, MARGERY ALLINGHAM on dialogue:

It is a curious fact that most writers of mystery or detective fiction seem to have a natural gift for dialogue. The explanation no doubt is that they *have* to, for in few other kinds of writing is the art so important.

Good dialogue is easier to read than anything else and its very shape upon the page invites the lazy eye, but even more valuable still from a crime author's point of view is its virtue as a space saver. A character can be revealed out of his own mouth more quickly than in any other way and the action of the story is not held up—or, rather, it does not seem to be held up—while it is done.

It is a fact that most readers of mystery stories read for plot but are held by, and afterward remember a tale for, the characters in it. Generations of obliging writers have found that the best way of giving their clients both what they want and what they think they want is by an intelligent use of dialogue in which both needs are catered for simultaneously.

Some authors write dialogue with astounding ease. Once the character is clear in their minds, they say, they sit back and "let him talk." But while this is obviously true, it is also pretty clear to the rest of us that a very complicated process is taking place in their subconscious minds while they sit around.

Mere reportage is of no use to the would-be writer of dialogue whose character remains obstinately dumb or when induced to speak shows a stilted address and a terrifying tendency to begin every sentence with "Well ...". No one who has ever taken the trouble to record living conversation can have failed to notice that when it comes to ordinary talk, very few of us succeed in saying what we mean at the first attempt and that most of us make a prodigious number of them. All but the few exhibit an affection for the same half-dozen words, and seldom do our remarks follow logically upon those of anybody else.

Perhaps it would be true to say that good written dialogue which aims at the natural rather than the scintillating is an idealized form of the real talk which would have taken place in the scene presented. It is idealized in the sense that each character knows what he has in mind and has no difficulty in expressing it. He listens intelligently to his opposite number, his reply refers accurately to what has been previously said, and by his choice of words he does not break the essential rhythm which alone creates the illusion of sound in the reader's mind.

Probably it is this rhythm to which those authors who "hear" their characters speak are referring. The English language when spoken fluently has a clear "tock-tick-tick, tock-tick-tick" rhythm which is so familiar to us that we recognize it as sound as soon as our eye meets it on the page. Heaven forbid that I should suggest that the young crime writer put his dialogue into blank verse, but I have noticed that one can achieve quite a remarkable degree of smoothness in one's dialogue by keeping the tune in one's mind.

As to the place of dialogue in the crime story, I should say whenever possible but always with the proviso that no character should be allowed to talk just because he can. A character in a detective story must do what no one in real life ever seems able to do, and that is *keep to the point.*

And now to implement these principles with some examples from another writer.

CARL G. HODGES, also on dialogue:

Basically, dialogue is talk, the talk of people. Therefore, for the same reason that you like to hear some people talk and it bores you to death to listen to others, so also do you like to read the dialogue of certain authors while that of others leaves you cold.

You may enjoy listening to certain conversations because the speaker projects his personality with his words; to others because of mannerisms that are fascinating to you; to others because of the colorfulness of their language; to another because of the fact that through experience you have learned that when he speaks he *says* something. The reasons why you like to listen to certain conversations are identical with the reasons why you like to read the dialogue of certain authors.

Dialogue should never be just talk on paper. Dialogue, every sentence of dialogue in any story, can also do one or more of the following things: (1) Move the story forward. Advance the plot. (2) Characterize or describe. Give a picture of character or environment. (3) Build conflict.

A sample of dialogue that moves the story forward is this bit from John Clare's smuggling-racket story from the October 30, 1953, *Collier's* entitled "Diamonds in the Sky":

Then the girl in the corner spoke, not to him, but to the elevator operator.

"Not too fast, please. Squadron Leader Cooper might get airsick."

Hank turned and looked at the blonde girl hugging an ermine stole around her shoulders. He stared for a moment without speaking. Nina — he shook his head. Perhaps he was still at Duxford; perhaps this was 1942. "Blondes away," he said softly.

Nina laughed lightly and stepped forward, slipping an arm through his. "You're impossible, Hank. You remember a very bad joke all these years, but you have nothing at all to say about me." She shrugged her shoulders. "After all, the last time you saw me I was sliding through the bomb bay of your Halifax over France to join the underground while you made corny jokes like that one. Blondes away, indeed. I think I hate you."

Hank put his hand over hers. "Nina, I can't believe it," he said.

She laughed and then said softly, "This is as far as we go, Hank. The elevator has landed."

"Oh, no," he said, shaking his head. "Oh, no, it isn't. We're going to have a long talk."

That bit of dialogue, clipped from the middle of Clare's story, illustrates the manner in which dialogue can be used to move the story forward and advance the plot. In it there are nine sentences which can be considered as narrative and fourteen which are dialogue. That is the ratio which holds true today in many successful stories. The sentences of actual narrative are so unobtrusive that the reader scarcely notices their presence.

Notice that in just a few words that dialogue also gives the reader a deft characterization of Nina, and builds conflict as well.

Another task that dialogue can perform is description and characterization. If a writer tells us in so many words that "Joe was six-one, had broad shoulders, weighed two hundred ten and one-half pounds, and was so big-boned and robust that everybody in the neighborhood was afraid of him, including the cops," he has given us a cumbersome and boring word picture. But if a character says these things in dialogue it comes across vividly. Thus someone might say: "Joe, you're built like Tarzan and you've got shoulders as wide as a barn door. But you always got a chip on 'em, hoping a cop'll knock it off, and give you a chance to throw your weight around. But remember, Joe. The law trims everybody down to size!"

Within those quotation marks the writer has managed an effective job of description and at the same time the speaker has added the characterization of two characters — Joe and his critic.

Aaron Marc Stein is as much at home with verbal pyrotechnics as with the simple sentences of a first reader, and in this chapter he shows that he writes as clearly as he thinks. In the course of his essay on style, he takes several side trips into literature and linguistics, explores a few aspects of technique, and hands out some sound, practical advice.

He writes in many styles — in the fiction field as George Bagby, as Hampton Stone, and under his own name. He has written in a stream-of-consciousness style, and he has written articles of scholarly criticism on art history and art criticism. He is a linguist with a classical background, and his use of words shows the value of a solid classical education.

20. Style

by Aaron Marc Stein

A writer's style, if it is to be effective, must meet three requirements. It must be natural to him, so much his own that he can handle it with grace and without artificiality. It must be acceptable to his chosen readers: readers confronted with stylistic hurdles they are unwilling to surmount are readers lost. It must be suitable to the material he has set himself to convey. Good writing is writing that gets the job done, and the job of a writer of fiction is to communicate to those readers he is trying to reach that story he is endeavoring to tell.

It is not purple prose. It is not fancy writing. It is not a parading of such words as live but rarely off the pages of a big dictionary. For a writer of crime fiction, the requirements that his style be acceptable to his readers and that it be suitable to his story are paramount. If a style that meets these two requirements cannot meet the first, then a writer would be well advised to turn to some other form of writing and leave crime stories alone.

In any crime story, whether it be mystery, suspense, chase, police procedural, or gothic, the writer, before all else, is selling action and suspense. He is writing for an audience that will stay with him only if he builds in them a hunger to know what happened, what is happening, and what will happen next. To accomplish this a writer needs a lean, agile, and efficient style. His sentences can carry no excess baggage.

If the crime writer's readers take any admiring notice of his style, it will only be in appreciation of the fact that he permitted them full enjoyment of the action and the excitements of his story without subjecting them to the irritation of verbal obstacles.

Marcel Proust, because he was Marcel Proust, because he was writing for an audience that wanted exhaustive exploration of every fine distinction and subtle nuance, and because he was describing an enormous complex of all but imperceptible slippages through which a new society emerged out of the decay of an old, got his job done, and superbly, by building intricate and monumental sentences into intricate and monumental paragraphs which rival in their complexity the human nervous system.

William Faulkner, dealing with a not dissimilar theme in a very different society, spread a verbal fog through which his stories moved from half-glimpsed meaning to half-glimpsed meaning and created a fascinating world of uncertainties and hesitations. Joyce, Nabokov, and Pynchon, delighting in verbal acrobatics, send their readers not only to one dictionary but to a polyglot library of dictionaries in pursuit of their word transformations and their translingual puns. But they are not read with the paramount focus on what happened, what is happening, and what will happen next. Their readers go to them for the pleasures and revelations of the word play. They are not annoyed by the word that stops them cold, they savor it. This is not to say that readers of Proust, Faulkner, Joyce, Nabokov, and Pynchon might not be your readers as well. But if they do come to you they come for a fast-moving story, nimbly told. Needless to say, the larger part of your readership will be made up of people who are yours because they want nothing but that from anyone.

We will assume, then, that a simple, quick-moving, efficient style is natural to you. That, of course, is not to assume that you brought it from the womb already matured, polished, and perfected. It needs developing. It needs working on; and, no matter how long, how much, and how successfully you have written, it needs unremitting vigilance.

How then is it to be matured, polished, and perfected? For a beginning there is reading and the reading must never stop. It should be omnivorous reading, including both good writing and bad. It should be attentive reading. If you enjoy a book or story or if you find one extraordinarily inept, go back for a second look at the parts that most delighted or most annoyed you. Take a hard look at the words. How did he get that over? Why did he miss? This is not to suggest that you attempt, in your own writing, to imitate prose that you like. But by examining the means by which other writers get their effects, you should come around to finding ways of making your own.

Study a foreign language, more than one if you can. Nothing sensitizes a writer to the music and the structure of his own language as does an ear for the different music and structure of another language. Do not, however, fall into the trap of peppering your writing with foreign words or foreign locutions. They will only be obstacles to the free flow of your prose. You want your foreign language to sharpen your awareness of the anatomy of English, not to replace it.

Now for the process of writing: A cliché of cultural snobbery refers to people who cannot read without moving their lips. Whether you are a writer who prefers to go with his first draft (a dangerous preference for any but a writer of long experience and hazardous for even most of those), or a writer who rewrites far more than he writes, let what you have written rest for at least a day or two, removing yourself as far as you can from what you may remember of what you meant to say. If you can work on something else before you go back to the manuscript, so much the better. When you do go back to it, shut yourself away in a room and read your copy aloud to yourself. I am without shame in confessing that I cannot write without moving my lips. The feel of the words on your lips and the sound of the words in your ears can tell you much about the quality of your prose. A sentence that doesn't speak easily is not likely to read easily. A passage that doesn't sound right probably needs revision, and there will even be times when you will find that you have made the necessary revision by the way you have misread it, that your misreading is what you should have had down in the first place. In any event, nothing will show up the awkward turn of phrase as well as listening to yourself read it aloud.

Another process to which you can profitably subject your manuscript before you let anyone see it is weeding it for adverbs and adjectives. Examine every adverb and adjective with hostility and suspicion. Do you need it? Will your prose move better without it? Try lifting it out of there. Not infrequently you will find that you have lost no necessary meaning and that your narrative moves faster. If the removal of your adjective or adverb leaves you no longer saying what you feel must be said, try other devices. It is always possible that a more specific noun or a more forceful verb will do it for you; and, if you can do it with noun and/or verb, you will be doing it with a more strongly focused impact.

Recently, when copyreading the clean copy I was about to submit to my publisher, I came on "the soft hiss of tires on the pavement outside." Has anyone ever heard a hard hiss? I have heard loud hisses. That's the polite way to summon a waiter in Spain. It's also a swan's anger signal. I've heard explosive hisses, the sound of steam released through a safety valve. If I were describing any of those sounds, I might need a modifier if I couldn't find another way of saying it, because it would be necessary to indicate that we had here no ordinary hiss. An unmodified hiss is a soft sound. The onomatopoeic word standing alone without the pleonastic modifier said it better.

Suppose that my original wording had been "the soft sound of tires." Removing the adjective and leaving only the unspecific noun would lose my meaning. Put the adjective back? No. Look for that more specific noun — hiss — or do it with a verb: "Outside, tires hissed against the pavement."

Have I sent you to the dictionary? I don't mind if I have. I am not trying to hang you on the ropes in hunger to know what happens next. If I were writing this in the hope of entertaining and exciting you, I would make every effort to do without the onomatopoeic and the pleonastic.

There is one aspect of style a writer is likely to find specially troublesome, and not because it is of itself too difficult to handle. It is an area in which a writer must beware of copy editors. Copy editors, all too often moonlighting teachers of high school English, tend to be hell bent on rooting out word repetitions. Word repetition, it is true, can give a passage a monotonous texture, but it is equally true that word repetition can be used to set up a compelling rhythm and to supply subtle emphasis. There is nothing for it but to read the passage aloud to yourself and trust your ear. The repetition may do what you want it to do. Then get tough. It's your prose and that's the way you want it. Copy editors are valuable for correcting your spelling and calling your attention to grammatical gaffes. But let them work on your style and you may find it reduced to homogenized ooze. On matters of style a good editor will almost always back the writer against the copy editor.

If your repetitions, however, serve no purpose and you find yourself saying the same thing twice, simple cutting takes care of that. Otherwise you look for synonyms, but this is dangerous ground. Never stretch for them; it ruins style and produces a ridiculous artificiality. The problem can come up in the writing of dialogue:

"Yes," he said.

"No," she said.

"I insist," he said.

"I won't do it," she said.

"But you must," he said.

"I don't have to," she said.

"You can't get out of it," he said.

"Well, if you'll do something for me," she said.

Impossible, isn't it? And right here all too many writers fall into the strained synonym trap.

"Yes," he said.

"No," she argued.

"I insist," he growled.

"I won't do it," she moaned.

"But you must," he commanded.

"I don't have to," she wailed.

"You can't get out of it," he warned.

"Well, if you'll do something for me," she coaxed.

Read that aloud to yourself. If it elicits from you anything but laughter or contempt, you have a tin ear. Obviously none of that is necessary:

"Yes," he said.

"No."

"I insist."

"I won't do it."

"But you must."

"I don't have to."

"You can't get out of it."

"Well, if you'll do something for me."

Doesn't that do it? The one "he said" at the start orients the reader to the direction of the first line of the exchange. In such a passage of rapid-fire dialogue, no reader will lose his way, because the pattern of alternation is reinforced by the context of the quoted words.

In a passage of longer speeches a reader might lose track of who is speaking, and in a situation which involves more

than two speakers he is almost certain to. Here you will have
to toss in identification for the speakers unless you can give
each character so strongly individual a way of talking that
you can expect a reader to identify each speaker by his peculiar style. You will find, however, that it is only in a few
special situations that you can expect your readers to follow
without guideposts.

In any but rapid-fire dialogue the repetition of "said" is
not to be feared. Monotony can be avoided by varying the
placement. It can follow one line of dialogue, and in the next
can be interjected at a natural breaking point in midquote.
Also there are other words that can be used without straining.
If it is a question, "asked." If it is a response, "answered."
If it is a tentative proposal, "ventured." "Moaned,"
"groaned," "wailed," "whimpered," "snarled," "growled,"
"snapped," "whispered," "thundered" — all are usable, but
only sparingly and only when they suit the content of the
speech. The snappiest of snappers cannot snap a 20-word
speech, and the thunderer must have reason for thundering.
Furthermore it must be a reason germane to the story you
are telling. You use the word to tell the reader something
he needs to know, not to spare him the agony of reading
the same word twice.

There are writers who work under the delusion that persistent repetition of one of these words can be used to establish
character. They have one character growl all his speeches
and another character whine all of his. The effect is weak
and quickly becomes absurd. In effective dialogue the reader
should sense the whine or the growl in the quoted words.

The handling of dialogue is, I believe, the supreme test
of a fiction writer's style. Dialogue is an artifact that has the
look and the sound of natural speech, but it cannot be a
reproduction of natural speech. Anyone who read even a
small portion of the transcriptions of the White House tapes
need not be told how much natural speech is halting, repeti-

tive, and unclear. It backs and fills. It breaks off and resumes. It is a bore to read and it is difficult to read. The writer must depend on his ear to give his dialogue the sound of nature, but he must depend on his imagination and his skill with language to chisel it down to readable form.

For that is the inescapable necessity of a crime writer's style. His story must not be a labor to read. It is well for it not even to look as though it might be hard work in the reading. Page-long masses of solid type look like work. The length of paragraphs should probably range between short and shorter.

In whodunit writing the handling of the conclusion sets the writer a special test of his skill. He wants to spring his surprise solution and then get out quickly. To follow the surprise with a lengthy exposition of the reasoning that led the detective to it is to end the story with anticlimactic boredom. The writer must manage an explanation that builds up to the revelation, and arrive there without giving himself away prematurely. He saves one crucial piece of the puzzle for the last and gives that to his readers along with the identity of the villain, and it needs to be a small and simple piece that can be presented in a few words.

In doing the exposition, furthermore, he will be wise to avoid dropping into monologue. He might cast it in the form of an argument, or break it up with explosions of action. However he does it, he must keep it alive. It must be drama, not a lecture.

To return to dialogue, there are writers (and some of them are even good writers) who have all their characters speak with the same voice, the author's voice. In crime fiction, I am convinced, it is not a good idea. I know of no more efficient and telling approach to the job of characterization than by conveying the individuality of each character through his manner of speech.

In most crime stories you are likely to have characters

who talk in street speech. The writer can avail himself of distinguishing contrasts: street speech, pendantic speech, simply correct speech, pompous speech. It is a temptation to give a character distinctive speech by having him talk dialect, but dialect is best handled as other types of speech are handled — by choice of words, turn of phrase, characteristic rhythms.

Leave phonetic spelling of dialect to the humorists. They can present a reader with an aggregate of letters that means nothing to the eye. The reader tries it aloud and his ear catches it, affording him a delightful shock of comic surprise. If you can play such jokes on your readers for occasional comic relief, all right; but be certain that you are not losing more by retarding the forward movement of your narrative than you gain by your little joke.

So much for details. In closing I give one general admonition. In every respect you must be specific. Telling your readers that a character is frightened doesn't do much toward ramming the fright home. Why not explore the physiology of fright? Select a few of its symptoms and have your character experience them — the dryness in his mouth, the pounding of his heart, the defensive rush of the blood to his body's internal reservoirs.

A British critic, preparing a learned work on William Blake, took some Blake engravings to Renoir and explained to the painter that Blake had insisted that when he drew angels in trees he was not drawing them from imagination. He had seen them. He had drawn them from life. Renoir's reported comment should not be forgotten: "I will not presume to say he didn't see them, but, given so rare an opportunity, he should have looked at them more attentively."

A writer works from his imagination, but he cannot look too closely at his imaginings before he puts them down on paper, since there they must appear in concrete reality.

Stanley Ellin has the distinction of having been awarded two Edgars for short stories, and one for a novel. In this chapter he goes deep into the process of creation and the dynamics of writing. Since he is knowledgeable about and interested in painting, he draws some interesting parallels between the two arts of painting and writing. Listen well to his ideas, for they limn out an essential approach to the entire craft of writing.

21. The Ungentle Art of Revision

by Stanley Ellin

When the day comes that computers will be programmed to write original works of fiction, there will be no need for revision of the printouts. Allowing, of course, for some IBM Fiction-Master X4 which, because its programmer was trained by a public utilities company, will keep turning out copies of page one until it is switched off.

Meanwhile, the need to revise any apparently completed draft of a novel or short story remains with us, as inevitable as death or taxes. It is not a glittering generalization, but an unvarnished fact, that there never has been, nor will be, a first draft of a fictional piece which would not be improved by revision. The amount of revision and degree of improvement might be arguable, but not the fact itself.

This is so because the writing of a fictional piece, no matter its length, is an ongoing process. I don't mean that in the superficial sense of events being described in progression. What I am saying is that the writer himself is caught up in the process. Fiction-writing is a product of the imagination, and imagination feeds on itself. No matter how sharply defined the story idea in the writer's mind when he first sits down to the typewriter, he is going to discover as he starts hitting the keys that nothing is coming out on paper quite as planned. A healthy, vivid, responsive imagination is what makes a fiction writer. And as soon as he gets to work, that imagination, almost as if detached from him, will ingest the lines he is writing and be led by them to start reshaping what is yet to come. This process of becoming, in effect, the instrument of his own imagination, takes place so naturally that the writer is usually unaware of it. What is happening is that he himself, the man with those ten fingers on the typewriter, is changing from instant to instant, moving further and further away from what he was during that period when the story idea was germinating in his skull.

A parallel to this may be found in another art: painting. A painter sets up a still life, visualizing in his mind the effect he wants to get on canvas. If he uses fixed lighting rather than natural lighting, the still life itself will remain unchanged from moment to moment. But not the painter. As an imaginative and creative human being, he is subject to the infinite permutations and combinations of emotional mood and mental considerations which his very first brushstrokes lead him to. With each stroke of the brush — indeed, with each tick of time — he changes. His finished work is, for this reason, a living work, which is why his picture, placed beside even the finest photograph of the same subject, will curiously diminish the photograph. A photograph freezes an instant of time; a painting miraculously and subtly reflects the passage of time in the artist's life while he was at his project.

So does a work of fiction, which, along the way of its creation, will take on a life of its own, for better or worse. Large characters may shrink, small characters expand to dimensions not planned for them. Nuances of plot start to devour the entire original plot. Scenes that one visualized so clearly before the writing now seem out of place altogether. New characters and new scenes pop up out of nowhere.

If the writer, intent on holding as close as possible to his original concept, becomes aware of this, he has the feeling of riding a particularly touchy tiger. But more often than not, as long as the words keep coming, he isn't aware of it.

In the end, only one thing is sure. The completed work may have gained or lost during its process of creation, but, to a smaller or larger degree, it will not be exactly the story one originally set out to write. The author may not realize it but it will be as new to him as it is to anyone else who may be invited to read the virginal manuscript. The difference is that this work is part of the author; it has been, so to speak, torn out of him, and he is going to regard it with intense affection and admiration no matter how anyone else may view it. The writer's eyes, while still bloodshot with the fever of creation, are not yet really able to focus clearly on his newborn creation. But unlike mothers, writers are not inclined to start by counting the baby's fingers and toes to make sure they're all there.

At this precise moment, any writer, if he has an iron will power and has managed to maintain some vestiges of sanity after having been locked up with his typewriter too long, should simply put away the manuscript in a drawer and mark off a date on the calendar when he estimates the eyes will no longer be bloodshot. At the expiration of that calendar date, he may then be able to take an objective look at his work. If so, he's now in shape to get out the blue pencil and do an effective job of revising it. The nature and extent of the revision will stem from the need to make characters consistent and plausible, to keep the narrative moving at a proper speed, and to play fair with the reader.

Beyond this lies what is often called a cosmetic job, most notably a whittling down of wordage. Admittedly, this hurts. Writers who will cheerfully add a dozen more pages to a manuscript in order to fill in a troublesome gap in its narrative will, when faced with the prospect of deleting a line of their deathless prose, fling themselves down and beat the floor with their fists. But — and here you may add to Unvarnished Fact

Number One this Unvarnished Fact Number Two — there never has been, nor will be, a first draft of a fiction piece which cutting can't improve. And, as I have slowly and grudgingly learned over too many years, it does get easier as you go along. Just a word here and a word there to start with — adjectives, especially, invite expunging — and then it begins to appear that this whole passage, even this whole page, is not really adding anything to characterization or narrative despite its brilliant phrasing, and so on and so on until one revels in the full masochistic pleasure of wholesale excision.

Even after all this, there still remains work to be done in the cosmetic department. The author of crime fiction may be allowed the wildest flights of fancy in his narrative, but when it comes down to those small facts which the reader can, and will, check out for himself, this writer is expected to be almost inhumanly accurate. Misplacing a landmark, routing a bus incorrectly, naming the wrong wine to accompany the fish — such are the catastrophes that must be insured against. If the editor happens to miss them, take my word for it that there's a host of hard-eyed readers and reviewers out there who won't.

And, contrary to a prevailing myth constructed from a very few unusual examples, sound grammatical usage and correct spelling do add to a story's charm, and, especially in the work of the neophyte, do weigh heavily in the editor's considerations. Granting that while sweating out his first draft, the impatient writer refuses to keep reaching for his Webster and Fowler, he should certainly be prepared to do the necessary reaching before the manuscript is mailed off.

If all the foregoing makes the job of revision sound as formidable a trial as the actual writing of the work, well, so be it. But, often, the only thing that seems that formidable is the writer's own inclination to feel that when he has typed *The End* on the final page of his project he has really come to the end. All along the way he has been lusting after those two words, and when he reaches them at last he is only too happy to take them literally.

Don't.

Because *The End* is only the beginning.

Anyone who can't, or won't, bring himself to believe that is, I'm sorry to say, a hopeless case and will have to be deleted.

A short time before his tragic death, Herbert Brean asked me to do a chapter on revision — on what Stanley Ellin in his article calls the cosmetic department. Here it is.

22. Once Over — Not Lightly

by Lawrence Treat

We all revise. The question is how, and when. To a certain extent at least, we revise in our heads. We may do it at lightning speed, selecting, electing, and eliminating, or we may do it slowly and painfully, telling ourselves no, not that, it doesn't sound right. The average writer, however, manages to get something down which he calls a first draft. Later on he looks at it and tries to improve it.

How?

There are no universal rules, but there are a few habits and guidelines that are common to the majority of writers. I put them down categorically, although nothing that concerns the craft should ever be stated categorically. Nevertheless —

Read and reread, and see how it sounds. The false, the awkward begin to yell at you. Read aloud, to friends, to a spouse, to yourself, and the soft spots, the bad writing show up. Read your draft with an eye to cutting. Never keep that clever, well-loved phrase if it doesn't belong. Slash it ruthlessly. Ninety per cent of revision is cutting. Have you said your say as simply as possible? Do you find any rhetoric, rodomontade, repetition? Cross it out.

Check your descriptions. Do they stop action? Have you described a room in detail, citing the bad taste of the furniture, cataloguing the curios and lamps and pictures, describing the blatant red of the couch when, for instance, you could have related every item to your character or your story? If you state that the curios irritate your protagonist, that the bad taste of the furniture annoys him, then you've both described the furniture and the character of the protagonist. You now have made him an esthete, or perhaps someone interested in all things, depending on how you angle his reaction. But more than that, you can key the description to the plot itself. The red furniture — isn't the material the same color as that thread which was found on the murderee's coat?

If there was no such thread, then go back to that earlier chapter and maybe it will be worthwhile inserting it, or some other clue that keys in with a description that was just dead space, and can now become an integral part of your story.

Check each scene and make sure it's not static. Does it start and end with the same emotion on the part of your protagonist? Is he angry at the beginning of the scene and still angry at the conclusion? If so, rewrite. He should develop or change in the course of each scene. He might, for instance, come in with hostility towards the banker or the mermaid, and in the course of the action lose his hostility and become sympathetic. Thereafter you might be able to use that change of emotion when your protagonist admits to someone else that he went soft. Thus you've written a scene that moves forward and builds up, and at the same time has shed light on your character and made him more real and human.

Check your dialogue, too. Is it in the idiom of your character? Consider, for example, the different kind of people who assent by saying *yes, yep, yeah, sure, surely, I think you're right, I agree, I think your notion is splendid.* Make sure not only that the idiom fits your character, but describe him in language consonant with his image. For instance, you might describe a lawyer as *dry as a document,* whereas a gourmet would better be called *dry as Chablis.* Let your lawyer *demur* to a statement, where the layman *objects.*

Check your character and place descriptions to make sure that there are no inconsistencies. Does Elswood Finnegan have blue eyes in chapter one, and brown eyes in chapter 12? It can happen, and often does.

Check your plot. Boil it down to a few sentences and see if it's logical and cohesive. Is it realistic? Have you gone off the deep end anywhere? Are there episodes that don't hew to the story line, that are extraneous and can be cut without any damage to your story? If so, you may have to throw out the better part of a book or story and virtually start all over again. Never be satisfied with anything but the best you can do. If a story is worth writing, it's worth writing well, and the habits of revision are the habits of your writing life.

Check for clarity. The lack of it is a major sin in your first draft, in your revised draft, and sometimes in the final, editor-approved version. It is a sin of writers and speakers. Too often the idea you have in mind is never quite put down. You think it's there, but it isn't. Sometimes your ideas are based on assumptions, on bodies of knowledge or areas of experience that your readers just don't have. What is crystal clear to you may be an opaque nightmare to someone else. Most arguments stem from the failure to communicate. How much more difficult to set down a sentence which will convey your precise meaning to thousands of readers with thousands of different backgrounds. I've read and reread sentences with but the vaguest idea of what the author was after.

How, then, can you be sure of putting across the image or idea that is so clear in your mind? You can't be sure, but you can try. Use the simplest language you can. Do you know the exact meaning of every word you put down? I've often looked up the simplest of words. Do you, for instance, know the difference between a *dale* and a *dell?* Does *drab* signify color or absence of color, and if a color, just what?

We make our living out of words. We should know their meaning, and we should use them properly. We should know when to use words of Anglo-Saxon origin and when to use a Latin-based vocabulary, and why to choose one as against the other. But above all, we should be clear, and to be clear often means to be simple. Don't show off your vocabulary at the expense of simplicity and clarity.

Watch out for repetitions of certain words or phrases. I once had a secret love affair with the word *march.* It was so secret that I was completely unaware of it, but my agent pointed out that my characters never entered or left a room, never crossed a street, never just went somewhere. They marched. He began counting the repetitions until I marched out of the office in horror. Only to march back in a few minutes later and thank him.

The areas of needed revision are endless and every writer has his own particular hang-ups. He is unaware of some of them, but the sharp eye and critical mind of an editor can often catch and expose them. If this is your first book, listen carefully to the suggestions of your editor and try to carry them out. Once you're established, listen just as carefully, but remember that this is your book and you have the last word. I know an editor, who is also a distinguished writer, who never tells me what to do, but makes suggestions and urges me not to carry them out unless I agree and feel comfortable with them. But such editors are all too rare.

Certainly the subject of revisions suggested by an editor is a vast, fuzzy area, and editorial reactions tend to be subjective. Some editorial ideas are valuable, and I always start with the premise that two heads are better than one, and that the writer should be grateful for the advice of a competent editor. It can be of practical help, specific and to the point, in which case all is well. It can be vague and yet perceptive, in which case the writer must guess what the trouble really is. But too often it is unnecessary and merely the meddling of a mind that can't let well alone, but has to make it worse, or perhaps merely different. For a number of editors are disappointed writers.

Of these, beware. But of all things, beware of the praise of a friend. It can be deadly, and often is.

Cutting is easy, isn't it? Particularly cutting somebody else's stuff. But your own? Well, all you have to do is take a heavy blue pencil, grit your teeth, and go to it. Yes?

Helen McCloy, novelist, one-time art critic, and Edgar winner for her mystery criticism, points out that there is an art to cutting, that it is a constructive, even creative, process, and that cutting can and usually does improve your story.

The first thing to cut is the beginning. Almost all amateurs fail to realize that you must begin a story in the middle, not at the beginning. A great deal must have happened before the curtain rises.

The first person who taught me about cutting was my mother, herself an author of short stories. I have never forgotten how she insisted I should slash the beginning of my seventh book, *The Goblin Market.* I had started it with five pages of writing about background and character, which I thought was simply beautiful. My mother cast these five pages aside and put her finger on one sentence near the bottom of the sixth page and said: "That is the beginning."

I raged. I refused to make the change. Next morning I woke up and knew instantly that she was right and I was wrong. So, today, the first sentence of that book reads: "Softly as he trod, Dona Calypso heard him." An opening sentence that starts many hares. Who is he? Who is Dona Calypso? Why is he afraid of her? What will she do now she has heard him? An opening sentence that would never have been achieved without cutting.

And how much better that opening is than a lot of boring stuff about character and background no matter how well written. Nothing is well written unless it serves the design. Good writing is not just a matter of words alone any more than good painting is a matter of paint alone. Good writing and good painting both are matters of architectural balance, design, structure. Cutting that ignores structure is butchery. Cutting that respects structure is surgery, which is particularly important in a mystery where so much depends on plot, clues, and other structural points.

"What else shall I cut besides the beginning?" you ask.

Simple: everything that can be cut. A story, a paragraph, even a sentence, is like an algebraic equation: anything that can go should go. Cancelling out produces the elegant equation.

23. Cutting: Surgery Butchery?

by Helen McCloy

Most revision techniques should be self-taug
hard work, trial and error, but cutting is an excep
rule. Here the beginner needs a few signposts t
his amateur's instinct to cut nothing.

There is an old, hard saying that should neve
ten: "No one is going to miss all the good thing
out."

A story is greater than the sum of its parts. A
distracts from the whole must go, no matter ho
that detail may be in itself. As architects used t
may ornament your structure, but you must n
your ornament."

Few writers can strip a story to essentials wit
and, without that stripping, you can't see the s
words. Sometimes, a short story or a lyric poem r
ten effectively in first draft, but almost never a
a book.

In writing a first draft, let yourself go in free
Spawn ideas, situations and characters, recklessly
sciously, at any length. Then you have something
is important for you can get design effects by
you cannot get in any other way. What would a
be if there were no holes in it?

"But *what* shall I cut?" asks the student.

What do I mean by "can go"? I mean anything that can go without damaging structure. How does one decide what damages structure? That is where the kind of judgment can unhappily be taught only by experience. I know of only one test that may help you to discover whether a passage should be cut or not: if it bores you, the author, while you are copying it, take it out. If it is vital to the structure, it won't bore you.

The first psychological hurdle to overcome in learning to cut is the beginner's reflex resistance to omitting even one of his own sacred words. The best way to do this is to teach yourself to cut so many words or lines per page on a purely mathematical basis.

I began my career as a writer working for newspapers and magazines where space was limited, where five thousand words meant 5,000 words, not 4,999 or 5,001. If your first draft ran 10,000 words and they wanted 5,000, you cut half of each page. In this situation a butcher will slash out whole paragraphs *en bloc,* or cut the top or bottom half of a page without regard for the effect on narrative structure. A surgeon will cut words only, without damaging structure.

There are various ways of performing such surgery. My own word-count usually runs ten words to a line, 28 lines, or 280 words, to a page. To cut half of each page means cutting 14 lines, or 140 words, from each page. If you cut one word from each line you have cut 28 words, which leaves 112 still to be cut. If you cut five words from each line, you have cut 140 words, a whole half-page, but you cannot do all of this mechanically. You must always allow for the fact that some pages, some lines and paragraphs, are more necessary to the whole than others. Dialogue lines consisting of one unnecessary word like "Really?" will be the first to go. Next you get rid of unnecessary prompting questions like, "What did you do next?" Adverbs and adjectives are always expendable. Keep a careful count of each word and line cut, so you do not cut more than you have to.

The next step is to read the whole page carefully while asking yourself with each sentence and each paragraph, "Could that go without damaging the story structure?" It is surprising how often whole sentences and paragraphs can go, and even more surprising how often the story is strengthened rather than damaged by such omissions.

Why is this? Because art needs limitations. Without them there is no design.

Now and then you will come to a whole page, or even two pages, that can be swept away without pain, a real bonus. Less often you will come to a whole page or paragraph or line so essential to the spirit or structure of the story that it cannot be cut. Then you compensate by cutting more from the next few pages.

If you can cut only 13 lines from page three, then you must cut 15 lines from page four or five. Always remember that if you cut one word from each of ten different lines on the same page, you have cut the equivalent of one whole line from that page.

If a paragraph ends with one line by itself, you can make your typescript look shorter by cutting that one word, but the story itself is not really shorter. It only looks that way, and the paragraphing in page proofs may be so different from the paragraphing in your script that it won't even look shorter once it's in print.

In my opinion you are not a professional writer until you can cut 28 pages down to 14 in one day without damaging story structure. Always remember that cutting has sweeter uses than compression alone. It is the best way to strengthen a weak story and the only way I know to turn a ticklish paragraph, or scene, into one acceptable to the reader. In my second book, *The Man In The Moonlight,* I had a four-page scene where a young man went into an epileptic fit. When I re-read the first draft, I was appalled to find that it was unintentionally funny. What could I do to make it what it was supposed to be, tragic? I cut those four pages to one-half page, and the scene was no longer funny. Brevity is the soul of much besides wit. It can keep you on the right side of the razor-edge between the sublime and the ridiculous.

Sometimes a student asks: "What about the opposite process? How do you expand a story? Turn a short story into a book?"

The best answer is: Don't!

Successful expansion is the most difficult of all writing techniques. If you have to do it, the Golden Rule is: DON'T PAD. Invent new structure, new characters, new incidents; don't just add new words. I had to do this job twice, and I pray I shall never have to do it again.

24. Avoiding Clichés Like the Plague

There are plenty of pitfalls, as well as pratfalls, in writing. How often have you picked up a book or a story and then thrown it aside and said, "Oh, that again!" How often has a blurb described a scene or a theme that you're sick and tired of? And yet, after reading a page or two (if you get that far), how often have you become absorbed in the story and been unwilling to put the book aside?

Clichés, then — what are they? Which ones should you avoid, and which ones accept philosophically, if not merrily, and certainly without fear?

We got the following answers to the question: What do you regard as the biggest single cliché — plot twist, type of private eye, twin brother solution, etc. — in mystery fiction today?

JOE GORES goes into the problem in depth, and he emerges with a gem of a treatise on mystery story writing:

No plot, in competent hands, need be a cliché. Any plot, in the hands of a bumbler, becomes cliché. Rather, to my mind, there are two central problems with a great many mysteries written today. First is letting your gimmick overcome your characters. I think a plot must grow naturally out of the interaction of your people, rather than the people being

fitted into the plot. It's easy for the writer to show
cardboard people being manipulated — or *event*
being manipulated — in such a way that the characters do things they really wouldn't do. In other
words, the people should be fully realized, not contrivances. Second, many mystery writers indulge
themselves in what I call "soft" writing. By this, I
mean they give us a street — any street. A car —
any car. But I want to see *this* street, *this* car. Stories
set in London must make me believe in London.
Or in San Francisco. Or in *this* pile of garbage, *this*
emerald brooch. Hard detail is what makes a story
believable.

Thirty percent of those who answered the questionnaire
agreed with Joe's first two sentences.

The late MARGARET MANNERS said:
Every blessed cliché has been used, and will be
used again and again. The good writer will use it
in a fresh way. Invert it. Turn it upside down, inside
out. There are infinite combinations possible. There
are no clichés in mystery fiction today, only tired
writers who haven't the strength to pull another rabbit out of the hat.

ROBERT L. FISH tells us:
Any plot twist, properly written, can be a good
book, and the neatest twist, poorly written, can be
a disaster. I think the greatest cliché today is to inject
politics — *i.e.,* the terrible Russians, the horrible
Chinese, as villains. Not only is it boring, but today's
enemy can be tomorrow's friend, which will date
the book.

PHIL RICHARDS comments:
Everything is a cliché. There is no plot device or

situation that isn't shopworn. People are interested in people, not in tricks, *per se.* Charlie Chaplin's dictum is inexorable: "Nothing transcends personality." You need the gimmick, the plot twist, but it won't sell your story. If the twist comes naturally out of characterization, it need be very slight.

ERNEST C. CLEMENT's comment is worth remembering:
They (clichés) come and go so fast that whatever I see now as a cliché will be gone by the time you read this.

Nevertheless — here are a few of the clichés which bother writers right now. Almost twenty percent of the questionnaires picked out the hard-boiled private eye as the biggest single cliché. As RICHARD MARTIN STERN phrased it:

I'm very tired of the two-fisted-super-stud-hard-drinking-hard-shooting-know-all-do-all kind of protagonist. Sex after beating. The protagonist has had his ribs kicked in. He's been booted in gut and testicles. He drags himself to his girl. She tapes his broken ribs, anoints his contusions, and stings his abrasions with a lavish application of iodine. The effect of all this first aid is electrifyingly aphrodisiac, and immediately he has at her. For him it may be a way of inducing his Florence Nightingale to give up on the iodine. For any reader who isn't delusional, it's the most boring of clichés.

JERRY JACOBSON says:
I never give a glance at mysteries whose artificial strength relies primarily on what I have come to identify as the Five B's, in any combination and for their sake alone: bullets, bodies, booze, blondes, and blood. Specifically, I refer to the hack private-eye detective tale.

The next blast, some 15 percent, took off on the formula gothic. HAROLD Q. MASUR merely jotted down his objection to the "blundering heroine in gothics."

EUGENE FRANKLIN BANDY spells it out:
The dumb biddy in the average gothic who keeps wandering through the gloomy old mansion for hundreds of pages asking "Why? Why? Why? Why? Why is all this happening to me? Can it *possibly* be that Rodney is trying to kill me?" Meanwhile Rodney has dropped a flower pot on her head and missed, tried to push her off a cliff and failed, fed her poison and had it regurgitated, and so on.

JANET GREGORY VERMANDEL objects to:
Blasé, cynical, downbeat, joyless, grey-hearted detectives, policemen, characters, who tramp through their creator's books, viewing life as an exercise in futility — and are thereby supposedly more *real*.

JULIAN SYMONS says:
Chases bore me stiff; I've had enough of innocent amateurs who beat the professionals; downbeat spy stories are now clichés where once they were fresh; masses of technical detail always leave me thinking that there should be a better way of passing on one's own knowledge.

Various other writers objected to various other clichés. MIRIAM ALLEN DEFORD's "pet dislike both as reader and writer is the final confrontation in which the murderer commits suicide." DONALD YATES is bothered by "the guilt of the most unlikely suspect." JAMES A. BRUSSEL cites "the overlooking of minute but significant findings — by the police." TIFFANY HOLMES and GEORGE D. LEON both object to the twin-brother solution. MARGARET LEIGHTON writes juveniles and finds that too many of them have the main character as an orphan. JULIE ELLIS cites the constant re-cap; MIRIAM BENEDICT dislikes italicized words which, often wrongly used, are supposed to give a foreign flavor. ELISABETH OGILVIE is tired of the double-agent gimmick, and SUSAN HOWATCH of amnesia bedeviling the hero. COLLIN WILCOX is annoyed by the victim who doesn't call the cops.

Some ten percent of the answers objected to dragged-in sex. GARY BRANDNER tells us his three bugaboos:

> Characters who talk exclusively in wisecracks. Private detectives who turn down fees. Embittered Le Carré-style spies.

MIGNON G. EBERHART says:

> Honestly, the thing that bores me is the old Sherlock Holmes formula: a brilliant detective and a stooge.

LILLIAN DE LA TORRE and JOHN D. MACDONALD object to amateur psychoanalysis. MacDonald says:

> I think the biggest and most insidious cliché in *all* fiction today is the tendency to apply the jargon of psychology, psychiatry, sociology to the interpersonal relationships of the people in the stories, and explain their behavior on the basis of these borrowed insights.

LEON WARE says:

> The worst cliché is the common practice of having "our hero" made a fool of just to prolong the book. Hell, if he's all that smart, he should have solved the murder by the end of Chapter I.

And finally, ROSS MACDONALD warns:

> An author's heavy investment in a narrator-hero can get in the way of the story and blur its meanings.

25. How Do You Handle Stumbling Blocks?

The next-to-the-last question sent out consisted of two parts: (1) In writing, what do you find is your biggest stumbling block? and (2) If you've found an effective solution or a partial one, what is it?

Some of the answers were far too personal, far too revealing to print other than anonymously. Lack of moral fibre, boredom, lack of any real ability, fear of rejection or of being unable to write — these were some of the themes that bothered writers. The solution, if there was one, was usually simple will power: force yourself, make yourself write. Then, like an engine that won't catch on a cold morning, once started, it usually hums along smoothly.

In general, the writing tribe has either suffered from the tortures of a Joseph Conrad, or else been slave to the meticulousness of a Flaubert. Either way, most of them have been hung up for a while and have had trouble forcing themselves to get down to work. Only a few escaped trouble and sprayed out their few thousand words a day and turned out a book or so per month with the ease of a six cylinder engine running on a full tank of gas.

A sampling of the various troubles of professional writers

will show you that, whatever your writing problems are, others have suffered the same agonies. For instance:

HILLARY WAUGH's biggest stumbling block is:
Working out all the little intricacies of the plot. I am not satisfied in that area unless every action has at least two different reasons for being and, if possible, four or five. My solution is to lie around and test and think and sweat and curse, and suddenly a breakthrough comes. In short, the solution to the problem is tackling it.

MIGNON G. EBERHART says:
Plot? I hate it! Solution? None; but sometimes a very clear analysis of character motivation helps.

Now listen to DANA LYON:
Plot, always and forever. And no solution, except that in recent years I have written about people's reactions to people rather than their reactions to events; my plots are simpler, the characters and motivation more fully developed.

Now MIRIAM ALLEN DEFORD:
Stumbling block? PLOT! Solution? I may work on a story in my mind for weeks; I think about it in bed before I sleep, and the people move forward a little and push the story with them. Sometimes talking over the possibilities aloud helps.

And LILLIAN DE LA TORRE:
Plotting. Solution? Develop the characters more fully, and they will act and interact.

DOROTHY SALISBURY DAVIS has the problem in reverse. Her trouble is:
The tendency to overplot — born of a fear of insufficient plot — and to go to incident rather than deeper psychological probing. Solution? Harder

work, deeper concentration, study of human reaction, and above all, better self-knowledge.

But to some writers, once the plot is in mind, their troubles have only started. STANLEY ELLIN speaks for most writers when he says that his biggest stumbling block is:

The first word on the first page. Faced with the need to at last press a finger on the typewriter key, I become aware that those beautiful words graved in my mind are going to look just terrible written down on that sinister sheet of white paper.

PAULINE C. SMITH, BRIAN GARFIELD, JERRY SOHL, LAEL J. LITTKE and many others agree that the most difficult thing of all is the simple act of getting started each day. Here are their solutions:

PAULINE C. SMITH:

Tear into the rough draft without worrying about syntax, form, or pacing; let the characters enter and act without agonizing over dialogue and motivation. Then tear the thing apart, revise and polish.

BRIAN GARFIELD:

Write anything. Get the thing going. You can always go back and write another first page or first chapter after you've established the momentum and flavor of the whole. In fact, it often helps to throw out your first chapter or two just as a matter of course, and take the necessary information out of it and feed it into later portions of the book in spoon-sized bites by way of summaries.

JERRY SOHL:

To start, first of all, regardless of anything.

LAEL J. LITTKE:

Forcing myself to sit down and start writing. It takes a lot of will power!

One wonders how any writer ever gets anything done. Plots are hard, starting is hard, and many writers bog down when they're halfway through.

VIRGINIA COFFMAN says it this way:

At page 150 or so I get a block through worry because the book isn't as great as I had hoped. Solution? Rewrite the synopsis of the last half of the book and keep rewriting it. The synopsis thickens logically with each rewriting, it rounds out the people and scenes, and the result is flesh, not fat.

PATRICIA HIGHSMITH's stumbling block is:

Not to have thought out the ending, or the last third of the book well enough. Solution? Nothing but thinking, which usually accomplishes nothing while one is trying to think, but later the solution will come, if a solution is due.

ERIC AMBLER tells us that his stumbling block is: "finding that what I am writing is beginning to bore *me*. Solution? The waste basket."

KATHLEEN S. RICH says:

The story is making progress, I know where I am headed as the outline is at my elbow, yet mysteriously, usually when I am least expecting it, I reach a deadlock. Nothing moves, nothing seems right. Something is needed but I don't know what.

Solution? I can't say it's perfect for all occasions but it has worked for me. I switch the viewpoint this passage is written in, and write it from one or even two other characters' viewpoints, which gives me new perspective and moves me along. These other viewpoints are not integrated into the story but the process moves me over the hump.

ENID RUSSELL, novelist and school psychologist, analyzes

the problem expertly. She tells us that:

> Blocking is a purposeful occurrence, meaning,
> "Take your time, you're not ready to continue,
> something has to think itself through first, in its own
> good time and without your conscious help."

> She adds that housework has its sole justification
> at times like these.

NANCY SCHACHTERLE speaks for many women when
she says:

> Time is my worst stumbling block. I imagine there
> are many housewife-writers with this problem. Since
> all aspects of meal preparation take up a good deal
> of a housewife's time, this is the area where I've
> saved most.

Solution? She plans menus carefully, shops as seldom as
possible, stocks up her freezer, and cuts down meal preparation by using a microwave oven.

DOROTHY B. HUGHES, distinguished writer and critic,
echoes Nancy Schachterle:

> Of course the biggest stumbling block is that there
> is too much else to do, particularly if you are run-
> ning a house. There's only one thing to do about
> these extra-curricular activities: ignore them until
> you have your stint finished. Or else get up earlier
> and knock them off before settling down to work.
> Or you can always clean house after your thinking
> slows down; it takes no mental activity to push a
> mop around.

FRED TOBEY covers the matter tersely:

> Stumbling block? Time available, uninterrupted.
> Solution? Write late at night, when all is quiet.

WILLO DAVIS ROBERTS cites:

> Lack of time and the needs of my family. I do

find, however, that the longer I stay away from the typewriter, the harder it is to get back to it. I can take a day off easily, but if I take four or five days, I keep finding excuses to do other things rather than get started again.

Solution? Write and write and write. Nobody ever pays you for the marvelous ideas in your head. I am convinced that nobody ever wrote a book because he had the time.

MIRIAM LYNCH and HELEN McCLOY, both of them conscientious workers, cite laziness as their main stumbling block.

PATRICK O'KEEFFE's biggest stumbling block? The first draft of a short story. Solution? None. There has to be a first draft.

LAURETTE P. MURDOCK's trouble: going off half-cocked, starting something before it has really jelled.

ROBERT L. FISH says he has many stumbling blocks. Among them:

When I finish a book, if I allow myself too much time before starting the next, I get out of the habit.

I haven't found an effective solution. I suppose the answer is to sit down and write every day, even if you throw it away later, but I hate to do it, and usually refuse to write if I don't know what I'm doing.

RICHARD S. PRATHER uses self-hypnosis and utter determination:

Coming up with a combination of ideas for a new book that really excites *me,* charges me up, turns me on. I have to believe, or temporarily con myself into believing, that I've devised a plot — characters, gimmicks, motivation, story-twist, something — that is *really* going to fly. Because if I'm not excited about and entertained by my own story, at least *while* I'm getting it down on paper, readers aren't likely to be much entertained by the thing once it's in print.

This isn't exactly a solution, but it's sometimes a comfort: Years ago I read (somewhere) the tale of the Stonecutter: An Observer watched the Stonecutter place his chisel atop a large granite boulder, and strike the chisel with his hammer; nothing happened, and the Stonecutter hit the chisel again; and again. Finally, on the one-hundredth blow, the great stone cracked wide open. The Observer, realizing it was not the one-hundredth blow alone that cracked the stone, but that one plus the 99 previous smacks, drew some wonderful moral from this, I believe.

Moral for writers: When the damn thing won't budge, hit it again.

PERCY SPURLARK PARKER comments on an item that may be of particular interest to the beginner writer. His stumbling block:

The trap involved in describing characters. "Mr. X. was tall, with blond hair and blue eyes; Mr. Y was short, with thinning hair and steely gray eyes." Although each description was different, they were given in the same manner. The reader is more likely to feel that he is going down a laundry list, rather than getting a description of characters.

RICHARD MARTIN STERN is honest and blunt enough to tell us what so many of us suffer from:

Stupidity. Mine. When I send in a first draft of a book and both my agent and my editor see the same weaknesses, and I think about it and see the weaknesses, too — then why in hell didn't I see them earlier by myself? One day if I can find him, I'm going to hire an idiot child of three to point out the obvious goofs I make.

Solution? That idiot child of three is my great hope.

JOHN D. MACDONALD's biggest problem is what he calls author intrusion. He says:

The reader does not care to be reminded that he is reading a book. Patches of gorgeous prose, or innovative and tricky structure, or unlikely internal monologues — all of these say, "Hey, look at me *writing!*"

The only solution is to put on another hat and read the whole book after you are quite finished, pretending that it is by someone who is parodying your style and exaggerating your faults. Cross out every distraction, mercilessly. When the final book looks logical, clean, tight and effortless, then you know you are worth your royalties.

Part IV dealt with how to write a story — and emphasized that the techniques for achieving a dramatic and suspenseful one are the same, no matter what kind of story you tell. Part V will survey some of the categories into which the mystery market is divided. Experts in each of them will offer comments and counsel about their respective areas. In the first of these articles, Phyllis Whitney gives the anatomy of the gothic. In the course of her remarks, she reveals both her affection for the gothic and her dedication to her own talent. With that talent and that dedication, she was bound to emerge where she did — at the top of her field.

26. What Do You Mean, "Gothic"?

by Phyllis A. Whitney

The American Heritage Dictionary puts it very well: "Of or pertaining to a literary style of fiction prevalent in the late 18th and early 19th centuries which emphasized the grotesque, mysterious, and desolate." Remember all those desolate moors in *Wuthering Heights?* Remember the hidden mad woman in *Jane Eyre,* and the sense of brooding mystery in both novels? Those were gothics, built on the foundation of the earlier *Castle of Otranto.*

Today a modern emergence of the gothic has developed into a genre of its own. Another name for it is the romantic suspense novel, which some of us prefer. Daphne duMaurier unquestionably started the modern version with *Rebecca* and *My Cousin Rachel,* and she has made her own public bows to Jane Eyre and Mr. Rochester. However, there was no great stir in the genre until the early 50s when Mary Stewart and Victoria Holt, encouraged by women who had the foresight to believe there was a good market for this type of book, made spectacular successes with *Nine Coaches Waiting, Mistress of Mellyn,* and other titles, building toward the explosion which was to follow.

Nevertheless, my own books, and the other occasional romantic suspense novels appearing in hardcover, were mostly ignored and seldom appeared in softcover. Then in 1960 one softcover editor, starting a romantic suspense series, called his books "gothics" and lightning struck. The softcover field opened up to all of us because readers out there wanted more, and they are still wanting more all these years later.

The well-written gothic is clearly one of the most lucrative and enduring lines in all hard- and softcover fiction. Where the standard murder mystery is fortunate if it sells 7,500 copies in hardcover, a first-rate gothic in the hands of an established and skillful writer will sell 100,000 in hardcover, and millions in softcover. Hardcover success is vital: it brings major bookclub exposure (and money!), as well as newspaper and magazine review coverage. But there is also a strong welcome for the *good* softcover original if it is not one of the cheaper imitators, which never sell as well.

Gothics are thriving in the British markets too, and in all languages around the world. They are written mainly by women for women, but a remarkable number of men readers also enjoy them, as I know from my own fan mail, and a number of men writers have hidden behind feminine names to cash in on what began as a success created and developed by women. A few men have even been brave enough to write them under their own names!

There is an excellent reason for the extraordinary popularity of romantic suspense. Exciting storytelling is perennially popular, and story is the essence of the gothic. The story must never be predictable, but build through an ever-deepening series of credible crises — often emotional — to an overwhelming climax and a genuine surprise at the conclusion that may fool even the seasoned mystery writer. Its appeal is honest entertainment and once-upon-a-time story magic, and readers surfeited with phony sex and violence welcome it. For gothics, like any other successful fiction, require absolute emotional involvement on the part of the reader with characters whose very real problems must be satisfyingly resolved.

Not that there isn't sex in these books. It smoulders in *Jane Eyre,* but it is subtle, not explicit: the imagination can often do a better job with the implied than with what is spelled out. Violence has its place, but not violence for its own sake, and its bloodier aspects are usually kept offstage. Anticipated terror is the bedrock of the story, and its promise must be fulfilled in a dramatic climax where death threatens. The "chase" scene is almost always essential, even more than it may be in a straight mystery.

As in the gothics of the last century, backgrounds are tremendously important. Often the setting is a real place. Foreign backgrounds are much in demand, as are interesting parts of the United States that have some exotic or different atmosphere to offer. As an American writer in a field crowned by English writers, I decided to make a virtue of background and atmosphere. I began to use foreign settings from the viewpoint of an American heroine, and readers seemed to like it. When I write about a place that is new to me, I read extensively about it before I travel there. Then I make copious notes on-scene and take color snapshots. When I write, it is always from the viewpoint of strangers to the locality — that being my own legitimate viewpoint — though of course people of the locality come into the story. On the other hand, if you can't make a trip to far places, the background can often be acquired through careful research. Superficial research always shows, I'm afraid.

Sensory details are important — what the main character can see, hear, smell, taste, touch. Not only the outdoors, but houses, rooms, furniture, clothes — everything that makes up *particular* background details — are richly presented, and enjoyed by feminine readers.

Period lends itself nicely to the genre, but it can be equally compelling in modern dress if the brooding old house, the atmosphere of mystery, the sense of a terrible unknown threat are there.

Of course we have romance, and the hero often looks to Mr. Rochester, Heathcliff, and Maxim de Winter as his ancestors. The writer plays variations as far as possible, and sometimes this brooding, dark-browed figure is the hero, and sometimes he's the villain, but we like to have him there. (On occasion he can even be blond!) He's apt to be pretty much a chauvinist, neatly captured by the spunky heroine.

One difference between the romantic suspense story and the standard mystery is that the police seldom put in an appearance. There may well be a murder in the past or in the present — and the fear of violence is always there — but if the police are called in, we don't dwell on procedure or on the details of detecting. It is the "civilians," not the police, who matter, and they don't sit around examining clues in the usual sense. Sometimes it is convenient to have the murder look like an accident, or even have it take place before the story begins, so we can get away from police business that may hold up the forward action. Gothics are true mysteries, but they are never detective stories. If there is any detecting, it's apt to be in the hands of a lady whose standing is strictly amateur, and she is usually out to solve the mystery of her own predicament.

The basic difference between the romantic suspense novel written for women, and the suspense novel intended primarily for men is that the male reader wants hard, fast, violent action and emotional turmoil may leave him cold. The female reader is often more interested in psychological conflict and the interplay of character. A suspenseful scene can take place between two people sitting in a drawing room if there is an honest confrontation involving an issue of substance, and if there is real uncertainty about its outcome. Of course there are scenes of exciting action in gothics too, but they are interspersed with people-conflicts that may not be merely physical. Happenings grow out of what the people are, as in all good fiction, rather than from outside elements.

The heroine usually starts out in a moment of crisis in her life, facing serious trouble and with a big problem to be solved. There must be something of importance at stake. She is often arriving in a new place with which she is unfamiliar — a place that is clearly to decide her future destiny. But beware of that plane about to land! We've all used that too many times.

In a sense, the gothic heroine is your truly liberated woman. Jane Eyre was fighting for independence and social change long before Gloria Steinem. Our heroine is courageous, struggling valiantly against great odds, although of course she may have moments of fear and trembling when she is quite willing to fall into the rescuing arms of the hero. Who of us isn't?

Which brings us to the everlasting pitfall that lies in the path of the gothic writer: how to get the heroine *into* trouble without having her seem foolhardy by rushing into situations of danger — as she must do — when if she had any sense she'd stay quietly at home and mind her own business, giving us no story at all. Personally, I fret under this objection of some critics. My heroines *are* reckless, headstrong, and determined to fight for what they want. I'd like to claim equal rights for them with the male heroes of suspense novels who are always going off alone into dangerous situations without anyone complaining. But there it is — discrimination — and so you'd better give that girl an awfully good reason for doing what she does and make it clear that she really isn't an idiot.

The heroine must be admirable, appealingly vulnerable to honest emotional stress — in a word, a true individual, or your reader won't care what happens to her. Though happy endings are in order, since this is intentional escape fiction, your heroine must deserve her reward at the end of the story, whatever it is. And she had better have her own goals and solve her own problems, even if the hero comes along at the climax to rescue her physically.

First person telling is favored to a great extent by most readers. Though there is no taboo against third person if you prefer it, the sense of reader participation is greater in the first person. Real feeling, real emotion can usually be better conveyed when an "I" is talking. Readers also prefer a single viewpoint: jumping from one character to another can break the line of emotional suspense in this genre, perhaps more than in others. But anything goes if you do it well.

As for technique, all the tricks and devices and efforts to fool the reader of any mystery story can and should be used. There must be suspense and a sense of immediacy in every chapter. Trouble is always *now,* and it must deepen in intensity. Obviously, characterization should have as much dimension as you can bring to it, and the writing should be the best of which you are capable. The gothic is for fun, it is entertainment, but the successes in the field are well written and please even the discriminating reader. In its own palatable way, the genre may even have some comment to make from time to time on current or past society.

To write gothics successfully, I believe you must enjoy reading them. These are not books you can write with tongue in cheek and one hand lashed behind your back, patronizing your reader. Respecting what you and others write in your own field, respecting your reader, is probably Rule One for any writer.

Will the gothic last? Well, it's been around almost as long as the novel itself, and within the boundaries of that mysterious and desolate landscape endless variations are possible. The rewards for the writer are satisfying: loyal readers and generous checks.

The softcover book started out as a reprint, competing in price and then superseding the pulps of the 20s, 30s, and early 40s. With the advent of new presses and new machinery that could mass produce, the paperback began to take over the mystery field. At first, it was considered a kind of second class book, much in the way the pulps had been regarded. You were a little ashamed to be seen with one, because books were Books with a Capital B, and Book readers were snobs.

In time, however, this changed; the paperback came into its own and drew some of our best writers. It demands a crisp, colorful style that is related to the humor and the lingo of the old West. For those who say that the paperback original is designed to appeal to the masses, let it be pointed out that Shakespeare, too, appealed to the masses. He wrote within a formula that demanded action and sword play, puns and low humor, and noblemen and noblewomen as heroes and heroines.

Dan Marlowe surveys the field, and his prose is as direct and hard-hitting in this article as it is in his books.

27. The Softcover Original

by Dan Marlowe

A change occurred in the world of books in the past few years. It used to be axiomatic that hardcover suspense publishers were the conservatives of the publishing domain, and softcover publishers the liberals. But the sex-and-violence revolution of the 60s and 70s changed all that. Anglo-Saxonisms from A to Z can be found in hardcover suspense at the rate sometimes of two examples per page. For the majority of the better softcover publishers, the rate is more likely to be two per book.

Explicit sex scenes are now found more often in hardcover than in soft. The often-mentioned bed-hopping life of softcover detectives of the past pales beside today's hardcover gumshoes diligently practicing their Freudian aberrations.

The reversal is as true of violence as it is of sex. In softcover suspense, the victim is as apt as ever to be brutally manhandled on a street corner, a dark alley, or a lady's boudoir. But when it comes to out-and-out formal torture scenes, rendered in clinical detail, they are more likely to appear in hardcover than in soft. If they do appear in softcover, the details tend to be elided or glossed over.

It can be misleading, of course, to make direct comparisons or distinctions between the hardcover suspense novel and the softcover original. It might be more instructive to compare the softcover original with its immediate progenitor, the daily newspaper, still the largest and fastest-selling publishing operation in the world.

Both are alike in terseness of presentation, economy of style, and direct attack upon the readers' sensibilities. Everything else, including character development, psychoanalytic insights, and authorial comment, is downplayed in favor of putting across the story.

Still, the beginning writer should understand first of all that in the case of writing the softcover original as opposed to writing the hardcover cousin, the samenesses can be more important than the differences. The differences are there, nevertheless.

Perhaps the prime qualification a beginner can have for the selling of softcover suspense is the ability to write action with impact. This means action verbs and action adjectives. It might seem elementary, but it is dismaying to see how often it's neglected.

Second only to the necessity for showing story-movement via action scenes is a facility for producing dialogue that literally crackles.

All fiction is a distillation of life with the monotonies ignored and the high points sharpened. The reader doesn't want to plod through the eight consecutive nights the detective stood in a rainy doorway, watching the lighted window across the street. The reader wants to see what happens when the light goes out and someone leaves the room. There is a refinement in the rendering of action for the softcover editor. It should be done with compression. Scenes shouldn't run on for pages, or perhaps even for paragraphs. For example:

> The door screeched open, and I went across the threshold in a sliding skid, shotgun extended. The two men were standing in grotesque attitudes of surprise. Moody reacted first and fastest. His right hand dipped toward the gun holstered on his hip. I touched off the shotgun's forward trigger. In the confined space the roar shook the cabin. Moody was still standing upright while half his head and all

his brains were plastered on the wall behind him.

Then he fell forward on what was left of his face.

An additional two pages of detail covering such a situation will in most cases weaken the effect, not strengthen it.

Compression is just as important where conversation is concerned, compression and another device: hyperbole. The *Webster's New World Dictionary* defines hyperbole as "exaggeration for effect; not to be taken literally." One thinks of John Gould's farmer in Maine who, when asked if the countryside had had much rain recently, shrugged and replied: "Stumbled over a sea serpent in the south forty this mornin.' "

Conversation cannot be placed on the printed page as taken from a tape recorder. In the writing of suspense, hyperbole can almost be considered a requirement.

Thus if the hardboiled detective says to the sweet young thing from whom he's trying to extract information, "You lie to me one more time, baby, and I'll kick your butt so high bluebirds can nest in it," (Philip Atlee), that's hyperbolic dialogue of the type a softcover editor might like to find on his desk some morning. Or if the hero wishes to assure a confederate that the latter is pursuing a correct course, the hero never says so. Instead, he might say, "Son, you can play that contract vulnerable, redoubled."

One reason for the softcover editor's insistence on strong action and snappy dialogue is the feeling in the industry that today's paperback readers are the same audience that watches TV. The reading has to be as effortless as possible, yet interesting, too. Once it becomes difficult to follow, or the pace slows, the reader will put the book down, and may never pick it up again. The reader must be continually rewarded with vicarious thrills for picking up your book in the first place.

Realism is another backbone of softcover fiction. Except in the case of deliberate fantasy or satire, care should be taken with the stated facts. This doesn't mean that it's sufficient to avoid having the protagonist fire 12 times from a 9-shot automatic without reloading. It means that editors look with extreme disfavor upon any action of the hero for which the writer hasn't properly laid the groundwork.

In other words, if on Page 208 of your story the hero jumps from the roof of a five-story building into a shallow dishpan of water, his ability to do so had better be set up by Page 15.

This gentle art is called foreshadowing, and its proper usage is important to the writer. Good outlining will avoid many of the pitfalls that find the author coming up to a situation where the hero might be required to do something for which he hasn't been provided the proper tools, but it's still a situation of which the writer should remain conscious at all times.

The wordage of his book is a target the beginner should keep in constant view. Most softcover suspense contracts are based upon the delivery of a 60,000-word manuscript. The ardent beginner, carried away by the fiery pace of his story, might deliver 65,000 angelically written words, but since the publisher is working from fixed expenses and a set cover price, the beginner's excess zeal will only succeed in running up the publisher's costs. The writer is apt to be considerably aggrieved at the editorial asperity with which such largesse is received.

Formulas should usually be avoided in the writing of fiction, but there is one in connection with wordage that can be helpful to the softcover beginner. Most typewriters using pica type will produce a double-spaced 28-line page. With a proper left-hand margin, it will result in ten- or 11-word lines. This produces, on the average, 300-word pages. The desired 60,000 words can thus be obtained with 200 manuscript pages. Twenty ten-page chapters, or ten 20-page chapters would be equally satisfactory. The point is that a framework is created that helps the beginner.

A handsome bonus for the writer of softcover originals, and one that should never be overlooked, is the viability of his product overseas. England, France, Italy, Germany, Sweden, Denmark, Norway, Finland, Holland, Spain, Greece, Japan, Brazil, and Argentina are all suspense markets which in the majority of cases have a larger per capita readership than the United States. Sweden, for instance, with a population of 8½ million, publishes softcover translations with first printings of 50,000. This contrasts with the 150,000 copies for a first printing in the United States, with its far greater population. Only the biggest names receive larger first printings. A softcover writer with a successful book in print in the U.S. can usually count on his book being published in half the overseas markets. Which half can vary from book to book, but if it includes at least one of the Big Four (France, Italy, Germany, Sweden), he will make more on his book overseas than from its first printing here.

Many softcover publishers are now actively considering buying more original fiction in order to avoid the fantastic sums they often have to pay for the rights to hardcover novels, not always with the happiest results. There is a wide difference of opinion about softcover originals. Some writers — as well as some readers — look down their noses at softcover originals. This is hard to understand since, when dealing with the better softcover publishers, the money is faster and there is usually more of it, except in the case of a hardcover blockbuster.

Several years ago a writer consigned the manuscript of a softcover original to his publisher, and after the usual nerve-wracking wait for a reaction, he received the following comment from his editor:

"In this manuscript you did something I don't see enough of lately; you struck a note, and held it."

Hardcover or soft, that's the name of the game.

Edward D. Hoch is not only a prolific producer of short stories in the mystery field, but the quality of his work is attested to by his short story Edgar award. He obviously flies through his plots with the greatest of ease, and he writes short stories because he likes them. This simple fact shows up again and again, and all the writers who discuss their specialties either say so directly or else clearly reflect it. In this chapter he touches all the bases — technique, character, mood, and money, with money being the home plate.

28. The Pleasure of the Short Story

by Edward D. Hoch

Once started, short stories do not always proceed as the author planned.

Characters grow and change, scenes shift, and occasionally the identity of the villain can surprise even the author. A writer must be willing to abandon his preconceived plot line if a better line of development presents itself. That's why I rarely use a formal outline, preferring to let the story carry me along. By its very nature a detective story must have a beginning and an end, but if the middle drifts off in a new direction, my originally planned ending might change.

In the detective short story there is little space for complex character development. The emphasis should be on plot and puzzle, though I do try to characterize my series detectives to a greater extent than the others in a story. Sometimes this can be done through dialogue, as in my Dr. Sam Hawthorne stories, or through involving my protagonist in a case that concerns him directly, as often happens with Captain Leopold. The funeral of a relative, a class reunion, an auto accident, a love affair, the arrest of a friend, even a police convention — all might involve the detective directly in the crime and give him or her some personal reason for solving it.

Another method of quick characterization is to tell something about your protagonist's past. No one exists without a past, and when none is mentioned, the lack of a fully rounded characterization can be most noticeable. The way a character thinks about his past, or what he says about it, can help shape him in the reader's eyes. Equally effective, as long as it isn't overdone, is the portrayal of a single trait — a personality quirk, a phrase often used — as in the case of Sherlock Holmes, Hercule Poirot, or Dr. Gideon Fell.

An increasingly popular feature of all mystery magazines is the crime-suspense story. Here, in contrast to the formal detective story, there is often space for character development. The rules are more flexible: even a beginning and end are not firm requirements. Thus a fine character study might well be written about a bank robber waiting in line at a teller's window, exploring his motives, his frustrations, his fears — and ending at the very moment of the robbery, the point where most stories would begin.

One of the distinct advantages of writing short stories as contrasted to longer works is that the author can explore a broad spectrum of people and places and themes in the period of time he might be devoting to a single long novel. I think this is what made the form a favorite with such writers of the past as Poe, Conan Doyle, and Chesterton. In an era when magazine income could just as likely come from lengthy serialization à la Dickens, these writers and others like them seemed most successful in the area of 5,000-10,000 words. It is, and always has been, an ideal length for the detective story, allowing for a statement of the problem, the investigation, the planting of clues and red herrings, and the ultimate solution.

Which brings me to the importance of clues and fairness to the reader. Such concepts may seem a bit out of style today, when so much short crime fiction depends upon a surprise twist at the very end, a denouement all the more effective because of its being totally unexpected by the reader.

No hint or clue is given that the protagonist is about to murder his wife, or that the friendly fellow on the next bar stool is a detective, or that the wrong person has been killed by the booby trap. It is the classic O. Henry ending, and no one ever handled it better than O. Henry himself.

In most cases, however, I prefer the story in which the reader is given a clue or hint well in advance of the ending. As a reader myself I find great satisfaction in spotting the clue and anticipating the author. If I overlook it, I don't feel cheated — I admire the author's skill! It is a game between us, the grandest game in the world. Is it possible that the decline of the pure detective story can be traced to today's hurried reading habits, where skimming leaves no time for a leisurely examination of clues?

New writers attempting the detective short story for the first time often run afoul of the great clue bugaboo. Clues are inserted with such a heavy hand that they almost scream their presence at the reader. The limited wordage of the short story calls for a great deal of finesse in the matter of clues, and I can offer no better advice than to read some of the classic authors like Ellery Queen, Agatha Christie, and John Dickson Carr. I find Carr especially to be a master at inserting clues into a scene of humor or outright farce while the reader's attention is distracted. It can be done, even in a fairly brief story.

I'm often asked by writers why I waste a good plot idea on a short story when it could so easily be expanded into a novel. Many mystery writers — S. S. Van Dine and Earl Derr Biggers among them — refused to write short stories about their series characters for exactly this reason. There are a number of ways to answer the question. With some authors, like myself, plots come to mind with relative ease. Start with a main character, add an unusual setting and a bizarre crime, and the plot begins to take shape almost before my eyes.

But more to the point, I "waste" good plot ideas on short stories for the same reason that I write them in the first place. It is the form best suited to a certain type of story. Poe could never have sustained the mood of "The Pit and the Pendulum" or "The Fall of the House of Usher" over an entire book. Likewise the enduring popularity of Sherlock Holmes rests on his short adventures. Some forms — the spy story, the gothic, the "caper" — are often most successful at novel length, where the author can gradually build suspense as he unfolds his plot. But the formal detective story, with its puzzle and resolution, is perfectly comfortable in twenty or thirty pages.

Another factor is the unity of an author's mood in the writing of short stories that is impossible in the creation of longer works — unless you're one of those rare writers who can turn out a novel in two weeks' time. This unity of mood, remarked upon by Graham Greene among others, shines through in the very best short stories, like the tales of Poe mentioned above. Simply stated, it means that the author is the same person at the end of the story that he was at the beginning. It can be an important factor in reaching the reader, in catching him up in the excitement of the story. This unity of mood can be a powerful weapon on the author's side, sustaining a short story in a way that would be impossible for a 200-page novel.

When I mentioned earlier my preference for the clued solution over the surprise ending, I did not mean to imply that the mystery short story should sacrifice the element of surprise in favor of strict fair play. Certainly the solutions of Agatha Christie and Ellery Queen show that surprise and fair play are both possible. But more than that, going beyond the simple question of *whodunit*, I think it's always best if some key element of the solution — the killer's motive, or his method — can be saved for the final paragraph, hitting the reader with one last surprise and leaving him satisfied.

This is especially necessary in stories where the solution involves a great deal of explanation. The detective can explain a portion of it, holding back an extra twist for the very end.

I've long been an advocate of series characters in detective short stories. From a strictly economic standpoint, a series character can mean a ready market for your stories. But one word of caution about them. It's all too easy to fall into a routine whereby the stories in a particular series begin to resemble the mediocre episodes of a weekly television crime show. You owe your readers more than that, and when you feel it happening, that's the time to try something unusual as a change of pace.

Some of my own most successful stories have been non-series efforts. These can be straight detective or crime tales like any others, but sometimes they're most successful when you try something really different in the way of setting. Thus an unnamed Arab kingdom can convert a fairly routine plot into something out of the Arabian Nights. Or a traditional war story can be made to seem like a tale of robbery and murder, simply by not fully identifying the setting until the very end.

Above all, writing a mystery short story should be a pleasure. If you don't enjoy writing it, chances are most people won't enjoy reading it. Choose your character, involve him or her in an unusual — even bizarre — situation, and then get him out of it, using his wits rather than mere chance. It's a formula for a pleasing short story.

Good luck with it!

William T. Brannon and his ten pen names might be described as a one-man conglomerate. Trained as a pulp writer with a pulp writer's technique and flair for the action scene, he has turned out thousands, yes, thousands of true crime stories. Here, sharing his know-how while he soft-pedals his talent for organization, he comes up with a survey of the true crime field that makes an expert out of everyone who reads this chapter. After reading it, all you need is to go out and do it.

29. Writing the True Crime Story

by William T. Brannon

A story once was described as "purpose versus obstacle in conflict." This also applies to the true crime story.

The purpose usually is to determine who committed a specific crime or particular series of crimes, generally murder. The obstacle is the suspect's efforts to avoid capture. The conflict is the work of law enforcement officers, whom I shall refer to as the police, in trying to find the perpetrator. The police work is the bulk of the story.

At last count, there were 18 magazines devoted to the true crime story in the United States. They buy at least 200 stories a month from freelancers. Other magazines of all types buy about 50 stories monthly. It is a hungry market, buying about 250 stories a month.

Outside the true crime field, about ten stories are bought by general magazines, such as *Kiwanis, The Rotarian, Coronet* and *Reader's Digest.* The other 40 stories are purchased by two groups — the men's magazines such as *Man's, Male, Men,* and *True* — and house organs like the *Ford Times* and the growing number of airline magazines *(Aloft, Sky,* etc.).

The 70s is a good time for the newcomer to break in. Many old-timers, writers who helped to launch the true crime magazines have died, retired, or drastically reduced their production. During the 60s, for example, I produced an average of three stories a week published under my own name and about a dozen pseudonyms. It was not unusual for me to write four stories for one issue of a magazine, and frequently five of my stories appeared in the same issue of one magazine. The editor was often short of material, and mine was always available. This is related to show the newcomer that there is a big market for crime stories.

Actually, an editor doesn't like to use more than two stories by the same author in one issue, and if good stories by newcomers had been available, he probably would have used some of those.

If you have material for a story, send the editor a brief outline. If he knows you, he may give you a firm assignment. If he doesn't but likes the idea, he will ask you to let him see it on speculation. If he doesn't like the story he will say so. This is something not true of most other editors; most true crime editors reply within a week and some by return mail or by phone. Several have that policy in paying too.

Example: I'm a staff writer for three monthly true crime magazines. Sometimes I mail a story on Wednesday, it is bought *and* a check vouchered on Thursday, the check is mailed on Friday and I get it on Saturday.

This is not designed especially for me. All checks are vouchered on Thursday and there's a good chance a check mailed the next day, you'll get it Saturday or Monday.

A majority of the mystery magazines have regular writers who are assigned specific territories. If your story is in one of these territories, the editor will check with his staff writer before he will give a newcomer the green light. Usually an editor will stick with his regular rather than take a chance on a beginner, because he knows he can depend on his staff writer. He has a magazine to fill with ten to 15 stories every month and that means deadlines. He can't take chances very often when he knows his regulars will come through. But that doesn't rule you out. When your query arrives, the regular may have died, he may want to slow down or retire, or it may be a month when he has more material than he can handle. You might be surprised how often this happens — and when it does, the editor will welcome a helping hand.

I assume that you are a beginning writer who wants to sell to the true mystery magazines. Most of what I say will be addressed to those writers. Having told you how you may get your foot in the front door, let's hope I can help you take that first important step that will lead editors to welcome a query from you.

The true mystery magazines want stories about current crimes. The closer the date of the crime to the on-sale date of the magazine the better. When a good story was more important than timeliness, an editor sometimes made up his magazine six months before the cover date, but the desire for recent dates has eliminated this practice. The resulting deadlines have given high blood pressure to many editors who wait anxiously for that last up-to-the-minute story to fill the book (*book* is trade jargon for *magazine*).

Some advice you doubtless have heard about other fields is just as valid in the true crime field. Before you submit even an outline, buy several issues of the magazines you want to write for and study the stories. They will show the sort of material the editor wants and how he wants it handled. Something else you should always remember: you are not writing for the reading public but for an editor. He or she is the first person you must please. If your story doesn't get past the editor, the readers will never know you exist. John Shuttleworth, early editor of *True Detective,* was asked the yardstick he used in deciding what stories to buy. He replied: "I buy the stories I like. I know of no other way."

An editor may tell you that "our readers want this." What he really means is: "I want this kind of story." He has no way of knowing what stories his readers want; the few letters he receives are far from a scientific sampling. So when an editor tells you what stories his readers like, you can bet he's telling you what kind he likes. That's the kind you should write.

When you get half a dozen issues of the magazine you want to write for to find out what is being used, you can be assured that the stories are the kind the editor liked or the best he could get. With that in mind, read all the stories.

I suggest you make a list of the states, sections and big cities where the crimes occurred. Maybe your locality or the area you can cover has no staff writer. The voids may be territories you can cover. A query will bring a reply as to which, if any, are not regularly covered. That's your chance to fill the gap. A completed story and a picture layout of a case in your area may well be the beginning of your career as a true-mystery writer. Pictures are important, because the editor uses from four to eight 8 x 10 glossies with a story.

You can't work alone, however — you need sources, and recent Supreme Court decisions protecting the rights of the accused before trial have made police less willing and able than they once were to reveal how a crime was solved. During the 40s, I hung around Chicago police headquarters so much that I was mistaken for a detective by people who didn't know better. Although a knowledge of police procedure is necessary for producing a good story, you would probably not be allowed the kind of freedom I was at Chicago head-quarters. Police work is the backbone of your story, though, so be persistent in your efforts to win their trust and you may be able to pry some information from them.

Early in 1970, the police department in Miami developed a videotape system for recording the image and words of the accused. The videotape is shown to the jury at the trial via closed circuit television. This type of evidence has been admitted by judges in Wisconsin, Florida and Illinois. It was first used in 1970 in the Dade County Circuit Court to convict a man who confessed on videotape that he had raped and murdered a beautiful blond housewife who also was a student at the University of Wisconsin in Madison. By the time you read this, the videotaped confession probably will have been admitted in courts in many other states.

The reluctance of the police to provide information has relaxed some but many policemen still are unwilling to tell a true-mystery writer how a crime was solved. Be persistent, you may be able to pry some information from them. A tape recorder is a way to record what a policeman tells you. Shorthand is another or you may have to use your own brand of taking notes.

Newspaper reporters have better sources of information than most other writers, and in newspapers you may find information the police wouldn't give you. Facts *per se* cannot be copyrighted, and you are entitled to use any appearing in a newspaper, usually in conjunction with what you obtained from the policeman.

Other sources depend on the locale of your story. In Illinois, every murder is followed by an autopsy and an inquest, with policemen giving many details of the investigation. Records of inquests are public documents in Illinois: the coroner is required by law to permit you to see them and make notes.

In most states, a suspect must be indicted by a grand jury before he can be brought to trial for a serious crime such as murder, but he is entitled to a preliminary hearing at which the prosecution will present some of its evidence and the judge will decide whether there is sufficient cause to bring him to trial. In states with preliminary hearings the testimony is a valuable source of information. You may get most of the important facts from newspaper accounts.

Most police have a public relations officer, and it will be to your advantage to get acquainted with him (or her). He may fill in some of the gaps, and in every case he will provide you with pictures of the officers and some of their equipment. Although few newspapers will sell you pictures, sometimes a newspaper has a contract with a local studio to furnish its pictures, and you may be able to deal with the studio. As a last resort you may have to ask your editor to get the pictures from a news service — UPI, AP, or NEA Service, which sells to magazines but not to writers.

However, if you are on good terms with the police, or if you can establish a friendly relationship, they may let you use your own camera — a $50 Polaroid is desirable because you can make two copies of each picture and give one to the policemen you are photographing. You may make pictures of all the offices involved, the crime scenes, the scientific equipment, closeups of places where evidence was found, buildings and cars involved, and most police departments will give you mug shots of the criminal.

There are many ways to get pictures of victims. In rare cases, a newspaper will sell them to you. If the victim was prominent, you may find his picture on the wall of the local chamber of commerce or country club. If he was young, you might find his picture in the high school yearbook. If you can't copy these with your camera, you may have to hire a local photographer to do it. If the victim, man or woman, was prominent enough, or if the case was bizarre enough, one or more of the news services will have pictures. Obtain pictures locally, it is always a good idea to get one of the chief, the sheriff, or the officer in charge. He will have to give permission for you to talk to the officers or take pictures and you should keep on good terms with him.

Another good source is an indictment. In most instances, an indictment will describe the crime and how it is believed that the accused committed it, both in considerable detail. An indictment, a coroner's inquest report, newspaper accounts, plus what you may have squeezed out of police officers, should provide you with enough material for your story. Since the Miranda decision, you have to squeeze every drop out of every source in order to get a good story.

One thing that will help you to produce a good story

is a knowledge of police procedure. In fiction you can get away with mistakes of procedure, but not in true crime. How do you learn your procedure? Study up on criminal law and get a police manual applicable to the area where you're working. And try to get details from the police themselves on how they work.

Most policemen like good publicity — and that's what you are giving them when you relate how their hard work, dedication to duty and cleverness solved a case. Until the Miranda decision many policemen were eager to have their stories told. They probably like the idea just as well now, but they don't relish a hassle with the high court, so they back off. But if you are persistent enough in your efforts to get acquainted, the police will come around in time — at least to give you enough information to enable you to write a story when it is merged with facts from your other sources.

Most true crime editors feel that any local color you can add will pep up your story. They also like brief biographical sketches of the police who did most of the work on the case. Usually one man stands out and he becomes your protagonist. When you talk to him, pump him for anecdotes and information about himself. When did he start in police work? Why? Does he like it? Does he plan to make it his career? If he has had several promotions, what were they and how did they come about? Does he have a family? How many children? What are his hobbies? What are some of his outstanding police experiences?

If you have done your homework — that is, if you've read the stories in several issues of the magazine you want to write for, as I suggested earlier — you will have concluded that the editor prefers sex stories over all others. Not pornography. Most editors keep such material at more than arm's length because they want their magazine to be fit for family consumption.

The sex story as it is used in the true-crime magazine is one in which a woman has a leading role, usually as the victim, sometimes as the killer or, if it isn't a murder story, as the victim of some other type of crime.

Although most true mysteries are murder stories, there are other types that can be made into exciting stories. These include kidnaping, rape, assault to commit rape or murder, spectacular bank robberies or any crime that is solved by exceptional police work. All the true-crime magazines carry the word *Detective* in their titles and insist on good detective work. The detective work actually is your story, and if you can't find out how the police solved a case, you might as well forget it.

Unlike newspaper stories, which tell the latest developments first and work back to the beginning, the true-mystery stories start at the beginning and continue in chronological order to the end. the end may be something like this: "After the jury had returned a verdict of murder in the first degree, Judge Richard Roe imposed a penalty of life imprisonment on John Doe. As this was written he was serving his sentence."

But if the defendant has not gone to trial, your end will read more like this: "On October 6th, the grand jury returned an indictment against John Doe charging him with first degree murder. Doe was arraigned before Judge Richard Roe on October 7th and pleaded not guilty. Judge Roe ordered him held for trial, and as this was written, no trial date had been set and he was held without bail in the county jail pending further legal action.

"But it should be remembered that according to the laws of this state, Doe must be considered not guilty unless he is proved otherwise through due process in a court of law."

The reason for running the disclaimer is to avoid a libel suit. Your story may point strongly to John Doe's guilt, and a smart lawyer may sue for damages, claiming you have caused great damage to John Doe, who hasn't even been tried. But that last paragraph tends to get you off the hook.

Lawsuits cause some editors to have nightmares. Two types of suits may be brought against a magazine publisher, in which the author and editor usually are named too, although lawyers know that most writers have little money. The lawyer is after the publisher, who usually has money.

One type is libel or defamation of character. The other is invasion of privacy, in which the plaintiff claims damages because his name was used without his consent. Nearly all are lawyer-inspired with a 50-50 split if the suit produces any money.

Truth is the best defense in either case. But there is no need for the invasion of privacy suit. It's the bystander, the man who comments on the case but does not appear in court, who sues for invasion of privacy. I get around that by using no actual names of anybody who does not appear in court, even though he may be quoted in the newspapers. If an individual has only an incidental part in the story, I identify him only by occupation. If he has a larger role, I give him a fictitious name. At the end of the story, a note appears:

> (Editor's Note: John Jones, Jim Smith, and Mary
> Doe are not the real names of the persons so named
> in the foregoing story. Because there is no reason
> for public interest in their identities, fictitious names
> have been used.)

Whether your story is written before or after trial, it is to your advantage to use fictitious names for all persons who did not appear officially in court. Right names of all persons mentioned in court records may be used without fear of a lawsuit, provided you reported what they said or did accurately. You need some sort of documentary proof — newspapers usually — because records of a trial are seldom typed. Instead, the stenotype record made by the court reporter is filed. The reason is that a court reporter charges a dollar or more per page for typing his notes of a trial.

There are exceptions, of course. If a convicted criminal takes an appeal, the complete record must be typed for the appellate judges and a copy is filed in the court records. Any record on file is available to writers. But in most cases the record is not completed until months after the trial, by which time the editor probably will have lost interest.

In most stories, especially those written before trial, it is important not only to have your facts straight but to qualify anything that might be challenged in a lawsuit by using such words and phrases as *alleged, allegedly, reportedly, allegations,* etc. If you quote any character in your story, it is a good idea to qualify that by writing, "the defendant was quoted as having said," or if you're quoting someone else, substitute his vocation for "defendant." Similarly useful phrases are "the prosecution charged," or "the defense claimed," etc. You should have some sort of documentary proof such as a news clip to back up any verbatim quote.

My dwelling on methods to avoid a lawsuit should not discourage you. I believe it is better for a beginner to know the pitfalls he may avoid at the start rather than to learn them the hard way — that is, having to defend a lawsuit. In the course of writing about 5,000 true crime stories, I've had a few suits, but they were all attempted shakedowns and I considered myself fortunate that the judges realized they were. The usual figure is $100,000 but once I had one for a million. When that came up, the man who was suing was a fugitive from justice in another crime and would have been arrested if he had appeared in court. I may not always be that lucky, so now I take the precautions I've just outlined.

When you sell to a true crime magazine, with a few notable exceptions, you give up all rights by signing an agreement. Most editors, however, will release other rights on request. If you can sell without releasing all the rights, it will be to your advantage.

I shall not try to tell you how to write your story except

to pass on this advice: several editors have told me they don't want fancy writing, but prefer a story told simply. You may find that this is not always easy to achieve, but it can be done if you work at it. And there's no better time to start than right now.

Here is a primer for the TV field. Want to know what your chances are? Want to know how to prepare a script, approach a director, what taboos to avoid? William P. McGivern, who knows the ropes intimately, offers some practical, down-to-earth advice. Not only does he have the answers to your questions, and gives them with the authority of successful experience, but he even asks the questions for you. A novelist and short story writer, he has written fifty-odd teleplays and ten film scripts.

30. Writing for Television and Movies

by William P. McGivern

The challenge of television first. Writing for the medium is demanding and competitive. Many word veterans, plus scores of newcomers from college writing courses, studio mail rooms, or wherever else fresh, ambitious writers come from, are all trying to get into this particularly tough, busy, high-income action because it is modern, provocative, and widely permeating. And because it is a material-consuming form that sops up story-telling talents that in former years poured into the huge mills of long-gone pulps, slick magazines, radio broadcasts, and newspaper supplements.

To be ruthlessly realistic, the odds are very high against writing prime-time television from anywhere that isn't within easy commuting distance of the big studios in Hollywood. In New York (except for the occasional dramatic special), there are soap operas, game and sports shows, news broadcasts, political specials, the weather, and so forth. But the half-hour, the hour, and the two-hour prime-time dramas and TV movies, those household-word accomplishments that joggle each other for sponsors' favors and for top places in the Nielsen ratings, are written and produced in and around the Hollywood locale. The sound stages, the technicians, the actors, and the producers are there. And so are most writers.

If your decision to write for television is firm, you must

be willing to watch it, to consider the TV screen as an instructor's blackboard. Television is a new and special craft or art form. If you find the tube uninteresting and/or a waste of time, then I suggest you forget about trying to write for this very modern medium because — whether you have the talent or not — you will lack the indispensable element of enthusiasm to bring to projects. The TV field is crowded with talent, writers determined to be seen and heard, and even the most comedic writers are also competitive and serious.

Do I hear any questions? I often do — from writer friends wanting to expand to the TV market, from letters in the morning mail from total but ambitious strangers, and from college audiences, often critical and cynical, but money-hungry, poised to take their chances on vying for assignments. And the questions often go like this:

"I have an idea for a TV show. What's my first step?"

Examine your idea. Is it a one-shot drama? Is it a springboard for a new series? Or is it a story for a series that is currently on the air?

Let's assume you want to try something for an established series. An idea may come to you from watching just one segment of that series. But better to watch several shows to get the full mood of the project and to avoid the possibility of spending labor on an idea which just does not fit the show's overall concept.

Now, the ideal would be to think out the story idea, then set up a meeting with the story editor of the series through your agent-representative. If you do not have an agent, a front-running expert specifically covering the TV scene, then you start with a handicap. It is a good agent's business not only to be familiar with story editors, producers, and so forth, but also to keep abreast of the progress of series — do they work through a stable of writers, has "your idea" already been used, are there still script vacancies on the program schedule, and is the show interested in trying new talent?

Besides arranging a work meeting or insuring that your script or idea is read, an agent is a valuable observer of the total TV scene. He also knows what new shows may be waiting in the wings, may be needing your talents.

"Can't I just write a script and mail it to whatever show I want?"

The major and independent producers of television refuse flatly to risk nuisance lawsuits by reading unsolicited manuscripts. Such scripts are almost invariably returned unread — in fact, unopened. On this, let me quote Wilton Schiller, a veteran creator-producer, who is also one of the most amiable and understanding men in the business and himself a writer, hence, having special creative sympathy. Says Mr. Schiller:

> In planning a series, many areas of general dramatic potential are examined. Out of these, stories and scripts will ultimately be developed. Thus, the amateur writer, or the professional not experienced in television, may send us, in good faith, a story about kidnapping. When and if at some later date we do a story about kidnapping, he or she may tend to confuse the particular with the general, and conclude that we have stolen his material. This circumstance has resulted in a number of tedious legal actions, very few of which have ever gone against the studios or networks. But it does keep us from reading unsolicited material from unrepresented writers.

However, I can suggest several ways around this hurdle. If you have a literary agent, he generally has an exchange-of-services deal with a Hollywood agent (just as most literary agents work with counterparts in the foreign publishing world). That Hollywood contact may be a member of one of the huge, powerful firms like International Famous Agency or William Morris, though I myself prefer a small agency with vigorous, personal attention. Ask your literary agent with whom he can put you in contact in the TV field, west coast preferably.

If you do not have a literary agent, try to use friends or even friends of friends with a studio or program contact. This needn't be the executive producer or the star, but *anyone* on the show from casting to the secretaries or dialogue coaches. The purpose here is to open a conduit through which a script can pass from your hands into those of a producer or story editor to be read and given serious consideration. A good agent is first choice. A good friend may help.

Syndicated columnist Dick Kleiner, a veteran reporter of the television and movie scene, has written that he is besieged by writers who want to crash the TV barrier. His suggestion is to try to interest someone at your local TV station in your material. Perhaps it can be used locally, or perhaps that station has an agent contact or even "a nephew over at NBC."

At this point, I can think of only one more recourse to get new material considered: pick a name from the credits of a given show, executive or associate producer, story editor or consultant, or the creator of the show, who has a continuing financial interest and may be especially alert to new thoughts. These names appear on the TV screen either before of after a given show. Write directly to the person of your choice, in care of the studio or company which has produced the film which you have seen and liked and want to work for. Tell him or her specifically what you admired about the show, the twists of plot, the shadings of the various characters and so forth. Be articulate and brief. Even in letter form, you are showing him how you handle thoughts and words. Then tell him you would like to write for the show, adding that you will send him a plot outline in a second letter. For a one-shot drama, send your letter to a producer whose product you have liked.

"Why not just send a script directly to a star you admire, one you hope will want to do your show?"

Because that unsolicited script might just go unopened, filed as fan mail, and all you would get for your efforts would be a nice, shiny nine-by-twelve glossy photograph of your favorite, machine-autographed.

"Anything special to keep in mind when planning that all-important plot outline?"

In preparing a plot outline (or do you want to gamble with your time and luck and send a completed script?), remember that the characters of prime-time television in a continuing series are carefully and critically honed in advance, shaped specifically toward a creator's and the producer's concepts, as well as the preferences and demands of the networks. Thus, it would be a waste of time to plot a romantic story in which Theo Kojak gets married, because the producers of the series may have already decided to keep him a sexy single. Let your story outline reflect what the series creators have already decided is essential and permanent in their shows. Otherwise, you're going to find yourself on your own, either creating a totally new series or writing for the wastebasket.

"How do most television shows get put together and sold to the networks in the first place?"

There is no inflexible pattern, but most of what we see on prime-time television gets there in one of the following ways: either an established television writer, usually someone particularly hard-working and determined, or an established hyphenate (a man or woman who wears two hats, as, for example, producer-writer) will conceive an idea for a series, research it, shape the characters, write an outline for the opening segment, and structure plot lines for three to six more potential episodes. Then, usually in cooperation with one of the major TV producing studios such as Warner, Paramount, or Universal (all major movie studios now have highly active TV operations on the parent lot), he will take the entire package directly to the executives at NBC, ABC, and CBS in charge of new programming. The networks then say yes or no. If the answer is yes, the network will order a pilot script. The costs of a pilot film, from writer's fee to production and actors' salaries, are usually paid for by the network, and the film is usually made at the studio which offered the idea.

Sometimes the creator of a series will write the pilot script; sometimes a veteran writer will be hired for that all-important first piece of film. Usually the creator of such shows will stay on with the series in some capacity and for some time, either as executive producer, producer, or story consultant, to insure quality and enthusiasm. Both the creator of the series and the writer or writers of the pilot film will participate financially, as arranged by contract, in every segment of the series that sees air-time. It is partly this high financial reward that makes the field so competitive.

If a network sets a time slot into its schedule, based on a successful pilot, the next step is to order a certain number of scripts. That number depends on the network's confidence in the concept of the show and the talent and credits of its writers and producers and, possibly, on the star of the series. A good idea and good scripts are more dependable criteria for success than an established star. Even the brightest can fade with the wrong material. It is my simple contention that the real stars are the good ideas, the good scripts, the good writers. In trying to create a series, however, it is completely feasible to work with the actor of your choice in mind and so inform your agent. In any case, the number of scripts ordered will range from 13 to 26 episodes.

Now the story editors call agents to ask for specific writers. (Here's the chance for an enterprising agent to suggest *new* clients.) Outlines of the proposed series will also be sent to agents and, if film is available on the project, producers and story editors will ask writers to screenings, and for personal briefings at the studios. Once again, these circumstances point out the obvious reasons why most TV writers live in or near

Hollywood. Not only is the writer readily available for conferences, to view pilots for which they might like to work, and so forth, it also gives him an excellent chance to judge a series he may specifically *not* want to work for.

If a writer is interested in what he's seen, he is invited to try out a plot for the series. This "try-out" can be a verabal or written presentation, depending on which is more comfortable for the writer and producer. Some writers project well vocally, with plot points skillfully aligned, dramatic peaks properly sharpened, and so forth. But most producers have suffered from an over-exposure to flamboyant story-tellers. They don't need verbal pyrotechnics, dialogue delivered in dramatic blasts, writers rolling on the floor to indicate their lines are uproarious lines. The story is the star here. You can't camouflage a lack of luster or originality with bombast and rhetoric.

Analyze your story in detail before your meeting. Make notes, if necessary. Name your characters. Concentrate on the strengths of your story. Tell it clearly and as effectively as you can. It is not a bad idea to rehearse your presentation. Tell it aloud to yourself or a friend. In short, be prepared.

But if you are not a confident and born storyteller, better put your outline on paper. However, if both writer and producer-editor have confidence in one another, verbal presentations are frequent and effective, because they can save time and allow for more flexible exploration of the story idea. Story conferences, incidentally, are no place for artistic rigidity and hypersensitive melancholy. Though you, as the writer, ultimately face the blank paper, television scripting is usually a cooperative effort in the give and take of ideas. Be ready for that in relation to your script.

If the producer likes the story idea, written or verbal, the writer's on the payroll. Contracts are signed and a check for "story money" is sent out while — if not already done — a written outline of the story is prepared for the networks.

The network or the series can still turn your story down, but once you have been assigned to write that outline, "story money" must be paid. Under the present Writers Guild stipulation, story money is seventeen hundred and some dollars for an hour show. But with the payment of that fee, your story idea belongs to the network or production company and, should they wish, they may assign another writer to do the script itself. However, if you are "cut off" from writing the script, the network or production company is obliged to pay the story money, plus 40 percent thereof.

"But if I am a creative writer, why can't I live where I choose and simply take my chances as a creative TV dramatist?"

Because TV is more than a typewriter and ideas. It is big business with a central location in and around Hollywood. TV companies are like sausage factories, and every episode is just one more link to be cut off, packed, and delivered to the public on tight deadlines. When last-minute rewrites are necessary, they are done with an eye on the clock, not the calendar. In a feature film, if the writer's back is against the wall, there is always time. The wall can be moved. In television, that can't be done as readily because at 8 p.m. on a given Sunday night, 20 million people are waiting for a scheduled show — one hopes, yours. Thus, producers want writers to be *available*. There is usually no time for conferences by mail. Story points or dialogue changes *can* be hammered out on the phone, but face-to-face story conferences are usually more productive and result in better shows. Which is why the pool of television writers is based chiefly in southern California.

"Any exceptions to this?"

One does come to mind. The writer who created *Owen Marshall, Counselor-at-Law,* was a professor at the University of Wisconsin, and commuted from Madison twice a month to supervise his show. While this was an intelligent and highly acclaimed series, it was on the air for just two seasons. I know of one New York writer, Arnold Horowitz, who flies to the West Coast for about six weeks a year, where he contracts for two or three TV assignments to be written back East. But Mr. Horowitz is a successful Broadway writer, and certainly an exception since there is little risk in contracting for his talents. Beginners would not be given such confidence and consideration.

We are talking, of course, about writing for television on a career basis, not just as a one-shot adventure. And to make a career salary, you must write from four to eight (depending on your tastes and needs) shows a year. When I lived on a farm in Pennsylvania, and flew out to Hollywood regularly to work on such series as *The Virginian, Ben Casey,* and *Slattery's People,* I had already written a number of books which had been made into movies, and I had a working reputation. Even so, it was several years and many shows later before I could take an approved outline back to the farm and complete the script there. It makes studios and producers insecure if a writer gets as far away as San Diego on a weekend. And in my case, I ultimately gave the whole operation a financial scrutiny. American Airlines and TWA, plus an assortment of motels, were making a larger profit than I. Now, by living and working in Hollywood, I am able to do the number of shows I want *and* have time for novels and other writing. It is very hard to be creative under the constant yawn of jet lag.

"But assuming it is simply not possible to take the chance of moving to the West Coast, can you suggest any other way of getting into television?"

Yes. Try to crack your local station or a station in the nearest large town. Write the program director, list your education background, special interests, writing credits, if any, and ask him for an interview and a job. There might be a slot in continuity of news, in sports, in preparing local specials. And, once again, working friendships can be useful chains in making other contacts.

"And if my main interest is in writing dramatic shows, putting my own stories into scripts?"

To keep yourself from floundering, wasting creative energies — and perhaps showing your work in an amateurish way — try to get a few actual television scripts to read and study for form and know-how. Real scripts are rarely available from studios because they are in such heavy demand by television writing courses on the college and high school level, so there is little use in writing studios to ask for them. Try instead a local college, high school, or the library. Even if the library does not have scripts on file, it is in a better position to request them from a studio for general rather than individual use, and most libraries are willing to perform such a service.

The story to be dramatized is yours, but a professional script will show you the accepted way to present backgrounds, locations, actions, emotion, all directions, dialogue, etc. A television script does not look like a stage play nor, even remotely, like a novel. Accepted forms are easier for professionals to read, and thus easier to accept.

If possible, it is wise to have a final script typed by a professional typist, someone who can make your script look as it should. Such services are not without cost, but let's assume you are promoting a potentially profitable talent.

Having read a few scripts, try to watch a TV show *creatively* to let yourself know just how it is constructed. And remember that most TV drama of the weekly series variety is middle-of-the-road entertainment, not *King Lear*, or *Death of a Salesman*, not purgative dramatic therapy. Sometimes, yes. But most television is story-telling entertainment.

So if there is a show you enjoy and would like to write for, do some homework on it. Watch it frequently enough to familiarize yourself with its characters, backgrounds, types of plots, etc. Let's examine *Adam-12*, a successful show that ran so long, we can presume most of us have seen it once or twice.

First, we note that it is a half-hour show featuring two young, clean-cut uniformed policemen, partners who operate a squad car together in Los Angeles County. Now the characters. Malloy is a bit more aggressive than his partner, Reed. In interviews, Malloy will generally take the lead, go through the doors first and so forth. He, we note, is played as the star, gets the most script action. Both men are brave, and there is not even a hint of corruption in these plots. Our heroes *can,* however, make mistakes. But they are upbeat — they never complain about the sorry lot of policemen.

The format of *Adam-12,* characteristic of this show but certainly not of all half-hour shows, is three vignettes and a tag. The three stories, sometimes four, are unrelated to each other except that they involve our young policemen, but the tag (the last page and a half of the script) usually reprises the first vignette.

For example: in an *Adam-12* I wrote, Malloy and Reed persuaded a woman to do her best to urge her son to come into the police station for questioning. They assured her that he had nothing to fear if he was innocent. Reluctantly, anxiously, the woman agreed to help. The subsequent search for the boy, his mother's pleas, his capture, wrapped up story number one. In the tag, we see the boy and his mother leaving the police station. They have a friendly, reassuring exchange with Malloy and Reed, and on this we FADE OUT.

Unless your memory is superior, you should watch the show you want to write for with notebook and pencil at hand. If you have never written for television, you must face the fact that it is — for you — a new medium. And even the most radical innovator is most effective if informed.

"It seems to me that a majority of popular shows today are about medical people or police and detective work. How can a writer get enough background to do an effective script?"

Medical and police shows are popular because both fields offer the ultimate in human drama, constant situations with life and death solutions. Every such major show has a technical adviser, usually a police officer or a doctor, working as an assistant, not only on correct wording in dialogue, but also on techniques, innovations in the field, and so on. If your script is accepted (or when you are given the go-ahead to work), one of these advisers is made available to answer your questions and thus give your scripts the ring of authenticity needed to satisfy producers and audience alike. If your work is in the speculative stage, devise your own dramatic situation, then try to research the background through the library or first-hand observation. Your own doctor, the local police, legal aid society, and others may be willing (and even flattered) to give you consultant time. Television is currently the single most popular source of entertainment in this country, and a few research questions put to a pro in his field can make him feel that he is almost a part of show business.

"Can you tell us something about the length and construction of completed teleplays?"

The length will obviously depend to some extent on what kind of show you are writing for. The camera burns up dialogue, while action requires much more screen time. Your script direction might read: "The armies clash," and a director could spend weeks fulfilling the requirements of that demand. But in televison a safe rule is that one page of script will average out to forty-five seconds of screen time. Thus, a half-hour show should run about thirty-two pages, and an hour show will run somewhere between sixty and sixty-two pages.

About construction: remember that your play will be interrupted five or more times for commercials, and you must therefore bring each act to a dramatic peak before the screen dissolves to the glories of detergents and deodorants. (Once again, use a favorite show or drama by a recognized talent as a form to study. Note exactly what occurs dramatically before each commercial.)

The intriguing, minute-long opening of most television shows is what fiction writers would call a narrative hook. In TV, it's called the teaser. A half-hour show will consist of a teaser and three acts. An hour show will have a teaser and four acts. The 90-minute made-for-TV movies will have either a teaser and six acts or six straight acts.

"What about camera angles, technical effects?"

You are the story-teller, the dramatist, and I suggest leaving technical advice to the director and his crew, which they prefer. TV and movie scripts are now written in what are called "masters." The writer blocks out master scenes and makes no suggestions as to movement of the camera *unless he wants to emphasize a plot point.* For example:

INT. MAIN TERMINAL KENNEDY AIRPORT — THE SCENE — DAY

We feature the normal flow of heavy traffic, customers lined up at ticket counters, sky-caps, etc.

THE SCENE — FAVORING JAMES MOORE

Moore, in his forties, strolls toward our CAMERA, casually scans a newspaper, apparently oblivious to the people around him. Moore, whose clothes reflect subdued but excellent taste, stops, checks his wrist watch, then glances at a clock on the wall.

Moore casually glances at a line of people waiting near a phone booth. Something alerts him. He reacts with narrowing eyes.

MOORE'S POV (point of view) — A UNIFORMED SOLDIER

The soldier, in his thirties, with two ranks of campaign ribbons on his tunic, stares tensely at Moore.

BACK TO SCENE

Moore strolls off casually, stops at a vending machine

whose front is decorated with mirrors. Moore puts a coin or two in the vending machine, glances casually at a mirror.

MIRROR SHOT — THE SOLDIER

With a hand in his pocket, he strides slowly, ominously toward Moore and we sense something implacable and brooding in the intensity of his manner.

What we have done here is move the camera four times. We start with an establishing shot of the main terminal building. We move to Moore. From Moore's point of view, we pick up the soldier. We move back to the scene, which includes Moore, and pan Moore to the mirror shot of the soldier.

The following scene is what we mean by a Master.

INT. RESTAURANT — ANGLE FAVORING MOORE — DAY

Moore is seated in a leather banquette sipping a drink. The soldier crosses to the booth, sits down facing Moore.

MOORE
Care for a drink?

SOLDIER
You think we can pick it up like that? Forget what happened to Gini?

As the scene progresses, it is the director's responsibility to move the camera from Moore to the soldier, or use a two-shot, or shoot from any angle in the restaurant he chooses.

In the first scene, we wrote directions that would cause the camera to be moved four times. The director might ignore our suggestions, but we have indicated to him that for plot purposes, we think it should be emphasized that Moore is under surveillance and that something unpleasant may be about to happen.

In the second scene, it's obvious that camera angles aren't

required, and even if the scene ran four or more pages, there would be nothing on the page but the actors' names and their speeches, a line or two to indicate their moods and actions.

In television, the writer and the director seldom work together on a script. In fact, the script you submit in January may not get to a director until March. Thus, it is imperative that you tell him by camera angles where you think the plot points are, and what emphasis you feel should be given to emotional conflicts.

"In doing teleplays, are there any taboos?"

Yes. You cannot show murder or visualize any anticipation of violence in a Teaser. That is to say, Network Practices do not permit a scene in which a gun is pointed at an unsuspecting man in a barber chair, and then dissolve to a first commercial. Production people cheat on this one by showing the gun alone, then the slowly opening door, then the unsuspecting victim.

Scatological words and sexually explicit language will not pass the network censors. Network Practices also forbid any caricature in a pejorative sense of ethnic groups, but decisions in this area can be rather whimsical. As an example, I wrote an episode for a now defunct show in which I featured a pair of heavies from Havana. The network didn't seem to mind that these characters were murderers and quite capable of selling their mothers to the gypsies so long as they "spoke nicely and dressed nicely." Those were the exact instructions handed down to me.

Certain censorships are related to the programs' time slots. In prime-time, before the children are in bed, standards are presumably higher and stricter — or perhaps more hypocritical — depending on your viewpoint in these. It is usually wise to write a script within your own standards of good taste. If your words or written actions constitute some "censorship violation," you will simply be told they do.

"Do you think the staple TV fare is likely to change in the near future?"

On educational television, yes. We've already seen some fine, innovative things there. In this area, what has been most successful has usually been borrowed from the meticulous and highly talented British who had centuries of theatrical activity and awareness behind them when television arrived. But I can't imagine much change in American commercial television: mystery, suspense, police and medical dramas, the legal scene, private eyes, family and ethnic comedy series, and, almost inevitably, a return of the classic western in series form.

Some of the finest dramas and specials have the lowest ratings because viewers prefer to watch weekly series to which they are not only loyal but addicted. The stunning dramatization of *Catholics* by Brian Moore from his own book, won high critical acclaim and a Peabody Award, but a miniscule audience. James Costigan's original and highly publicized television play brought Sir Laurence Olivier and Katharine Hepburn together in a deeply romantic story called *Love Among the Ruins*. But since the show scored only a 55 rating that evening, it's clear that audiences across the nation offered the celebrated lovers a dismal degree of privacy.

"Are courses in television writing available?"

Yes, most colleges and universities and a few big-city high schools, have expanded their journalism and communications schools to include all aspects of writing for television. Some of these courses are good, to be sure, but too many are taught by instructors with little practical experience in the field. Universities near the base-centers of Hollywood and New York are able to use working dramatists, directors, and producers as guest professors. Others must still scrounge for working scripts to study, use textbooks written by non-pros, and function without the proper lab-experience atmosphere that could make television study and work the vital, experimental challenge it should be. However, I believe a course in television writing can be helpful to almost any writer if he keeps firmly in mind that he cannot "graduate" into the field without ultimately doing his own original, salable material in loneliness, determination, and/or joy — at his own typewriter.

Now let's take a look at the movies. I think it will be useful to concentrate on American movies — which, of course, means Hollywood. Whether they are made in Spain, or England, or on location in Jackson Hole, Wyoming, American movies, as a rule, are financed in New York and written in Hollywood.

But do take note of the changes in the industry: as recently as 1969, the major studios and the independents, the whole movie-making world of Hollywood-Los Angeles, had an expensive staff to search for material that could be made into movies.

Story editors in Hollywood and New York covered all the Broadway plays, best-sellers, magazine stories, and creative events abroad. Their staffs dug through paperbacks, newspapers, biographies, and autobiographies on the hunt for material which could be adapted for movies. Almost every piece of fiction and dramatic nonfiction printed in English was read, synopsized, and considered as a motion picture possibility. Also, the studios were staffed with producers, directors, and writers who could make this conversion as speedily and effectively as possible. These studio staffs were permanent on-the-lot, on-the-payroll personnel.

That's all over now. The majors and independents have dismantled their story departments. With the growth of television entertainment and the financial crunch of the late '60s, the studios began demanding that producers and writers and directors gamble along with them on projects. Which means short money up front and a participation, with luck, in the profits. The studios have removed themselves to a large extent from their former editorial role. They are now waiting for a producer and/or a director to come to them with a good story idea or completed script, and often with prominent actors committed to the project. Thus, the studios keep their up-front financial involvement to a minimum.

The great sound stages that for decades dominated the movie studio lots are now used to film television shows, as well as the occasional movie.

Getting a picture made today can be a tedious, discouraging job. Then, you may ask, why bother with it? My answer would be that film is the major innovative art form of the Twentieth Century. It is challenge.

To write a good screenplay, you must have an eye for the visual, and not only the talent, but the distinct preference, for story-telling in terms of pictures instead of words.

There is a familiar example of how a veteran screen writer made visual the boredom and banality of a marriage: Husband and wife enter elevator. Car stops at a lower floor, and a smashing young blonde enters. Instantly, the husband removes his hat. You need no words to tell an audience that the singing and the gold have gone from that particular marriage.

Keeping this in mind — the *visual,* the story told in *pictures* — will give you clues on how and where to look for backgrounds and plots that suit themselves to the big screen.

Certain areas of human enterprise, though possibly rich in emotional or spiritual turmoil, are so buried in physical monotony that the camera would likely be at a loss to make them interesting and dramatic. For example, the professional tribulations of a landscape gardener probably would not make a good film. But the same approach to a mobster, a trapeze artist, a gigolo might be fascinating.

An injunction that would apply to most writing: write your screenplay about something you know, or something you are eager to research. Or something that reaches the point of truth within your imagination. And be prepared for a long stretch of creative work. Few screenplays, adaptations or originals, can be put on paper in less than three months, and it often takes much longer — a definite commitment in creative time. As a personal example, I am currently working with Director John Frankenheimer who will direct a book of mine called *Night of the Juggler.* Here is the timetable on that one: the book itself took about fourteen months to write, with six weeks out to polish a screenplay for John Wayne and another six weeks to do an hour-long *Kojak.* The first draft of the screenplay for *Juggler,* written for Producer Jay Weston, took about three months, based entirely on the novel which already existed. Then Mrs. Frankenheimer joined our project. So far, we have spent three weeks, with another ten days of conferencing on the horizon, discussing what aspects of the novel-screenplay he would like to film. Incorporating his many ideas into the final script will take another four or five weeks. Screen writing is never fast, never easy. In fact, it is an especially sensitive art form produced and scrutinized twice — once on paper as an entity, and once again examined, loved or rejected on the big screen.

Directors and producers are seldom in agreement about how they want their scripts written. Certain directors are insulted if a writer puts an adverbial demand on a line of dialogue. Like:

MOORE
(angrily)
Kiss off, you idiot . . . .

Directors will tell you that the actor will try to act the adverb rather than the dialogue. They will tell you that it is their function to lead the actor to emotion. But certain lines might be totally enigmatic without a bit of verbal direction from you.

Producers and directors can also disagree about the de-

scription of characters, rooms, clothing, etc., in the script —
sometimes for budgetary reasons. I described a dress that
Joan Crawford would wear in a picture as being "a slender
poem in black." And Producer Bill Castle told me to cut
the description on the grounds that Miss Crawford would
instantly be thinking Balenciaga instead of Sears. Personally,
I think it is useful to include a description of rooms, cars,
gardens, clothes, etc. Also, I find it helpful to describe characters in some detail and in flattering visual terms if I am writing
about the leads. Although the description may not fit the
actor eventually chosen to play the part, he will nonetheless
have a general impression of what the character looked like
originally in the eyes of the writer. A bit of telling description
also helps to sell the studio or the independent producer on
the general excitement of the script.

There are two newsstand or subscription sources that can
keep you abreast of what is being bought and produced in
the movie world: the daily and weekly *Variety* and *The Hollywood Reporter.* Purchase of properties such as novels, finished scripts, etc., are usually announced in these papers as
are the assignment of writers to film projects and some information about subject matter involved. A study of these trade
papers can keep you informed about ideas already in the
works and thus save you time and creative enthusiasm that
might otherwise be wasted on trend ideas. For instance, after
the wild success of *The Sting,* an original screenplay idea,
the market was deluged with con-men stories, few of which
reached the screen. *Easy Rider* brought a stream of youth
and drug culture pictures, and when the vogue palled, a lot
of writers were left with dead scripts. If you know what are
currently visible screen projects, you can better judge which
of your own ideas to develop.

Once you have your script written (an original or perhaps
an adaptation of one of your books or short stories) and feel
reasonably confident that you have visualized it (told it in

moving pictures), get it off to your agent. If you have specific actors, or a favorite director in mind, make a note of them for your agent.

If you don't have an agent, there really isn't much point in mailing your script unsolicited to a studio. You should try your best to get published in magazines, books, paperbacks — anywhere that will make you attractive to an agent, because it's he who will give your film script a chance to be seen by packagers and studio executives.

As many writers are contributing their scripts to universities and colleges, it shouldn't be difficult for you to get hold of a script written by a professional to familiarize yourself with mechanical forms of writing for the screen. A two-hour screenplay should run from 125 to 135 typed manuscript pages. The price you may be offered for your manuscript can range from $5,000 up to six figures.

To write films, you must start with the pleasant chore of becoming a serious film buff. See all the movies you can afford, in theatres and in film societies. Watch for the classics that turn up regularly on the late, late shows. After this exposure, you will begin to be aware of how master craftsmen visualize everything from action to interior monologues and tell their spellbinding stories in moving pictures. Yet films are still a new art form, constantly changing, constantly in flux, always offering a welcome challenge to newcomers to create their own magic.

Bill Pronzini is a versatile writer who is equally at home writing short stories or novels — or the monthly bulletin of the Northern California chapter of the Mystery Writers of America. Living so far from the main TV markets, he needs an agent, and he has one good enough to have sold to the movies and most of the foreign markets.

PART VI: AFTER YOU'VE WRITTEN
31. On Agents
by Bill Pronzini

Among the most frequent of all questions a professional writer is asked by his as-yet unpublished brethren, are those having to do with agents: *Is an agent really necessary? And if so, should I obtain one before or after my first sale? What other services does an agent offer besides selling manuscripts? What commissions does an agent take? How can I be sure an agent is reputable? If I decide I need an agent, how do I go about selecting and approaching one?*

These questions, and their answers, are important to the budding author of mystery and suspense fiction; a clear idea of the pros and cons of literary representation will make it easier for the new writer to decide whether he or she will benefit by using an agent. What works for one writer does not necessarily work for another, but the choice should be made early in his career.

Is an agent really necessary? And if so, should I obtain one before or after my first sale?

Most professional crime-story writers agree that an agent is invaluable, because he can offer a great many services which the writer is usually unable or unwilling to attend to himself. The beginner, however, may or may not need representation in order to make his or her first sale, depending on a number of factors.

The unpublished mystery author working in the short story form is likely to do as well on direct submission as through an agent. Most literary agencies will not handle short crime fiction, except by established professional clients, for the simple reason that the market for short stories is severely restricted. There are, unhappily, only a handful of magazines devoted solely to mysteries, and only a few slick-paper periodicals which use occasional stories of crime and suspense. Fortunately, magazine editors will always read every submission that crosses their desks, whether it comes through an agent or from an individual, either professional or beginner; good mystery shorts are at a premium, and editors are constantly looking for fresh talent. Short fiction is still the easiest way for an unpublished mystery writer to break into print, and to stay in print, and because of this, new authors would perhaps do well to submit their own material at least until they make a sale or two.

The beginning mystery novelist, on the other hand, might have a better chance of selling his or her work through the offices of an agent. Because the market for crime and suspense fiction is limited where beginners are concerned, professional competition is fierce, and a number of hardcover and paperback publishers have all but ceased reading unsolicited manuscripts. But agents' submissions, from beginners as well as from professionals, are always read. In addition, an agent deals with publishers every day of the week and knows what type of material each editor is currently looking for; he can take your manuscript to exactly the right market the first time — and he can generate enthusiasm for your work through his personal contact with editors.

Catch-22, however, is that most literary agencies will not take on an author unless he or she has made at least one professional sale; the problem for the unpublished writer, then, is finding a reputable agent who will handle his or her work. There *are* still, of course, some publishers who read and encourage direct submissions from new writers, and who are as likely to buy one as they are to buy an agent's submission. Quality mystery/suspense fiction will always find a home. If you decide to submit directly to a book publisher, you should first study the market reports listed periodically in the various writer's magazines and yearbooks like *Writer's Market;* these reports will tell you which publishers welcome unsolicited manuscripts from beginners.

Another factor to consider in deciding whether or not an agent is necessary is your own critical requirements. Some new writers feel the necessity of a professional reaction to their work *before* it reaches an editor; if you are one of these, be wary, although an agent may be able to supply you with such a reaction — and perhaps offer constructive criticism which might strengthen the work through revision, thereby making it all the more salable when an editor finally does see it. Again, the individual writer must decide what is best for himself.

What other services does an agent offer besides selling manuscripts?

An agent negotiates publishing contracts so that the writer's best interests are served. He obtains the highest possible advance payment for material, and the best possible royalty rates. He sees to it that the writer's published work is distributed to foreign agents and publishers, television and movie people, and other potential reprint or subsidiary outlets; and when a sale is made in one of these areas, he handles contracts and monetary negotiations. He passes on current market information, letting the writer know which publishers are buying what kind of material. He arranges, if the writer so chooses, special assignment projects such as novelizations of movie and television productions.

The good agent, in short, is a friend, adviser, critic, and business partner; he does everything humanly possible to advance the writer's career and to earn for his client the maximum payment for his or her literary efforts.

What commissions does an agent take?

Every reputable agent takes the same standard commissions: 10 percent of the writer's earnings on all sales in the United States (novels, short stories, movie and television rights, reprint rights); and 20 percent of the writer's earnings on all sales to foreign countries (10 percent for himself and 10 percent for the agent he works with abroad). These may seem to be rather substantial, but for the services rendered to the writer, the percentages are quite equitable.

How can I be sure an agent is reputable?

Generally speaking, almost all literary agencies are reputable or they would not be in operation. But as in any other large business, there are a few who unethically abuse their good office. Membership in the Society of Authors' Representatives, although not essential, is as good a guarantee as you can get of an agent's reliability.

Certain agents offer, for a fee, to revise the writer's work in order to "make it salable," or to revise the writer's work for a considerable percentage (as high as 50 percent) of the money realized from a potential sale; avoid these agents, and avoid literary representatives who demand larger-than-standard commissions from beginning authors on domestic and foreign sales.

A few agencies charge high reading fees for manuscripts submitted by unpublished writers, which fees are not refundable should the manuscript be subsequently marketed and sold; only a small percentage of reading-fee submissions are ever taken out to market, and usually all the writer receives for his money is a generalized, one- or two-page critique. This reading-fee practice is frowned upon by the Society of Authors' Representatives; and most professional writers believe that, except in special cases where the individual feels he or she must have a professional reading and is unable to get it any other way, there is little value in paying large sums to have your work evaluated.

The important thing to keep in mind is that the policies of a reputable agent will always conform to established practices, especially where commissions and fees are concerned. In addition, a reputable agent will never use pressure tactics — hard-sell ads and letters, promises or guarantees of any kind — in order to obtain reading fees or other remuneration from unpublished writers.

If I decide I need an agent, how do I go about selecting and approaching one?

The Mystery Writers of America, Inc., the nationwide organization to which the vast majority of mystery and suspense authors belong, has a list of recommended agents which they will gladly supply on request. Of these recommended agents, a few are willing to work with promising beginners without charging reading or evaluation fees. Others will agree to represent new authors on a contingency basis, which means that they will handle a certain amount of work (such as one novel) in the hopes of selling it, but that if it does not sell, they will no longer represent that writer's future efforts.

Since each agent operates in a slightly different fashion, manuscripts should never be submitted without querying first. Should you decide to contact one, send a letter requesting a statement of policy with regard to the representation of unpublished writers, and briefly describe the kind of writing you want handled.

Far too many writers have signed their first book contracts humbly and gratefully, in tears of joy that blinded them even to the large print — and lived to regret accepting the terms of that first wonderful contract. Every literary gathering is littered with the debris of stories about writers who sold all rights to that first book, and then went on to fame without fortune — the fortune going to the publisher.

There is less leeway and less room to negotiate when you sell a short story to a magazine, but short story rights can become valuable and you should sell nothing beyond rights to that first shot — first North American serial rights. I've often made a half-dozen subsidiary rights to a short story, mostly to anthologies and foreign markets.

With your first sale, you're a pro and you'd better act like one. You should be a businessman as well as a writer. If you can't handle your business, then get an agent.

Harold Q. Masur, novelist, attorney, and businessman as well as MWA's official toastmaster, gives you some sage advice about contracts, and grounds you on the practical side of writing. Besides following his advice, be sure to have the wherewithal to sell those future, subsidiary rights. Get 20 or 30 extra copies of every book: you'll need them to sell in Europe or to various reprint outlets. Get enough tear sheets of that magazine story of yours to have copies available. If you have only one copy, have it xeroxed and keep a few of those copies on hand. Set up a filing system and know what rights you've sold and what rights are at liberty, and have that material available to you at all times. Even if you have an agent, you may change agents and be unable to get possession of your records.

It's a delight to be part of the writing world, to know agents and editors and to go out to lunch with them, but their job is to make money, and you're basically just a literary property. So — protect yourself at all times!

32. Legal Aspects
by Harold Q. Masur

Publishing contracts are long and complex documents, and an attempt to cover all their various provisions in detail would be more appropriate in an article for legal scholars. I would like to offer here some of the more important suggestions and a few guidelines.

Virtually all publishers offer a printed contract form with blank spaces to cover individual situations and for negotiating specific terms. When you receive this contract, those spaces will already have been filled in. Unless you are an established author with a proven track record or represented by a tough bargaining agent, you may be inclined to sign the contract under the terms offered. On the other hand, you would probably find most major houses moderately flexible and responsive to reasonable demands.

Since trade editions frequently sell only a modest number of copies, your most important source of income will derive from subsidiary rights, most conspicuously from paperback sales. The traditional 50/50 split on such royalties between the trade edition publisher and the author is no longer sacrosanct. The established author should be able to vary the division in his favor, starting on a sliding scale which would give him minimally 60 percent of the second $10,000 and 70 percent of all sums over $20,000. An author should also hold fast on a similar division of income from such additional subsidiary sources as book clubs and abridgments for newspapers and magazines.

It is understandable that a new author will often make concessions depending upon his need for publication. But, clearly, if you have what appears to be a likely winner, even in the case of a first novel, publishers will certainly offer more favorable terms. If you lack aggressiveness and bargaining skills, then by all means get a literary agent or an attorney well-versed in this area to negotiate for you.

For purely pragmatic reasons the following exhortations seem advisable:

Copyright in the book should be secured in the author's name. This is accomplished by a notice on the reverse side of the title page stating the word "copyright" (or its symbol, a small circle with the letter "c" inside, although most copyright notices employ both), the date, and the name of the author. Thus: *Copyright © 1976 by John Smith.*

The copyright laws are explicit and rigid, and failure to print this notice will throw the work into the public domain. Either omission or error is inexcusable. In this connection, it would be wise not to rely on the original publisher to renew your copyright after its initial term. Do it yourself. Write for a renewal application to the Register of Copyrights, Library of Congress, Washington, D.C., and return the completed application with the appropriate payment.

You cannot secure a statutory copyright on an unpublished manuscript, but you are protected by a common law copyright which accrues to you simply by the act of creating original material. Once the manuscript is published (which means printed and distributed), the statutory copyright becomes effective.

If you're the anxious type, afraid that your material might be appropriated by an unscrupulous editor or publisher (which is highly unlikely), and you would feel more secure with some measure of protection, I suggest that you send a wax-sealed copy of the work to yourself by registered mail, thus establishing its date, and then keep the letter or package intact until such time as you may have to prove a common-law copyright.

Most contracts provide for the delivery by the author of a satisfactory manuscript. Thus, the publisher retains the privilege of ultimate rejection. In that unhappy event, the author should be allowed to retain the advance in exchange for his considerable investment in time and talent. He was to engage on a mutual venture with the publisher, who should likewise accept some share of the risk. If he insists on reimbursement, the author should keep at least 70 percent of the advance.

At a minimum, royalty payments should provide for 10 percent of the retail price on the first 5000 copies, 12½ percent on the next 5000, and 15 percent on all copies in excess of 10,000.

Many publishers, not all, will try for a share of first serial, motion picture and television rights. Resist. An author is entitled to keep 100 percent of all income derived from these sources. If, however, the publisher negotiates the sale of such rights on the author's behalf, acting as his agent, then the publisher is entitled to the standard 10 percent commission.

There should be a provision in the contract requiring the publisher to pay over to the author his share of monies collected from such subsidiary sources not later than thirty days after their receipt. It is, after all, the author's money, and considering the fact that statements are rendered only twice a year, it should be drawing interest in the author's bank account rather than the publisher's.

All contracts should provide for reversionary rights. Once the book is out of print, the author should be able to terminate the publishing grant. When a book stops producing royalties, it serves no economic purpose. It would be even wiser to recapture your rights once the book fails to earn a specified annual royalty.

If the book is also out of print in paperback, the author should terminate that license, too. But since the original paperback grant was probably made by the trade edition publishers, you should request the paperback people to notify them formally that such termination is effective, and you should preserve a copy of this letter for your files.

These reversionary rights can be extremely valuable; once recaptured, you may be able to interest another publisher in bringing out a new edition. And if you negotiate such a grant with a paperback house, you will not have to share this income with anyone.

Costly and troublesome problems occasionally arise because of option clauses. These clauses give the publisher the right to publish the author's next book, on the theory that the publisher has made an investment in the author by advertising and promoting the first book and the publisher should be able to reap some of the harvest if subsequent books are successful. But what if the advertising and promotion are negligible or non-existent? What if the book is permitted to die? The author is still bound by the option clause.

Few publishers will permit you to delete this clause. Try anyway. If unsuccessful, it would be wise to insert the phrase "on terms to be arranged," and then add an automatic cutoff period giving the publisher a specific time (thirty days would seem adequate) in which to decide whether he wishes to accept your terms or not.

The Mystery Writers of America, the Society of Authors' Representatives, and The Authors Guild have all prepared model contracts. Any of these would serve as a helpful guide.

On several occasions we have received inquiries about the similarity in plot between two stories, with our correspondent wondering whether a plagiarism suit would not prevail. Legal precedent seems heavily weighted toward the principle that ideas *per se* are not protected by the copyright laws. The protection does extend, however, to an author's development and treatment of an idea.

To cite a few examples of material apparently developed from almost identical ideas, observe the following:

The Tower by Richard Martin Stern concerned the destruction of a skyscraper by holocaust. Same idea: *The Glass Inferno.*

Stanley Ellin published a novel, *Stronghold,* in which a gang of criminals holds a family and their friends for ransom. Remember *The Petrified Forest* by Robert Sherwood? *Desperate Hours* by Joseph Hayes? All use the same central notion. And yet, in treatment and development, all are as different as the authors themselves, each of whom saw his theme through the unique prism of his own individual imagination.

In *Rendezvous In Black,* by Cornell Woolrich, a prospective bride is killed when someone among a group of celebrants tosses an empty whiskey bottle out of a plane. Vowing vengeance, her heartbroken fiancé sets out to kill all the passengers aboard the plane. Compare this with the film *The Bride Wore Black,* directed by Francois Truffaut, in which a man, celebrating with his friends, drunkenly fires a gun through a window, the random bullet killing a bridegroom as he emerges from a church across the street. His avenging bride sets out to kill each member of that group.

One final example. John D. MacDonald wrote a novel called *The Last One Left* in which a private yacht is wrecked and its passengers slain in order to conceal the theft of a large sum of money aboard. Likewise, Hammond Innes published a novel in which a freighter is presumably sunk in order to conceal the theft of gold bullion in its hold.

So we see that two authors, working independently, may create stories that look strikingly similar. But the author who arrives in print first, with a proper copyright notice, cannot automatically bar the second writer from publishing his work.

In order to make out a proper case of infringement the first author must show not only access to his material but a significant amount of similarity in language, characters, and story development. And even this may not be enough if the similar material is such that it would normally occur in any story dealing with the same subject. For example, a novel with a college background would by its very nature involve students, professors, and administrative personnel. So be wary of plunging into a plagiarism suit. If the court decides that your case is frivolous and without merit, it may direct you to pay costs and counsel fees for the defendant.

A title may not be copyrighted unless it is so unusual and distinctive that it is closely and unmistakably identified with a particular work and its author. Thus, *Catcher in the Rye,* a book which continues to sell year after year, would certainly be injured if someone were brash enough to appropriate its title. The protection here would fall under the rule of "unfair competition" rather than under the copyright laws.

In regard to privacy, you may use the name of an actual living person in a passing reference, but only for the purpose of establishing background and not for commercial exploitation. And be cautious about statements that may damage his reputation or hold him up to public ridicule. In works of nonfiction, where public figures are concerned, the restrictions are somewhat relaxed.

33. Tricks of the Trade

The last question on the questionnaire asked for one-or-two-sentence pearls of wisdom on the general subject of the best tricks of the mystery trade as learned over the years. On the whole, writers objected to the suggestion that there *were* tricks of the trade. Over and over again they reiterated ALAN K. YOUNG's response to the question:

> The best trick of the trade I've learned over the years? Simply to keep at it, to keep plugging away.

DON VON ELSNER tells us:

> The best trick, I think, is to reconcile yourself to the cruel fact that there is no trick, and that you wouldn't want to use it if there were. Tricks are for tricksters. Writing is for writers.

And J. D. FORBES says:

> The trade has been cheapened by "tricks." There is no substitute for simple logic.

There was, however, plenty of advice. Twenty percent of the answers emphasized the importance of creating sound, believable characters; about ten percent, the necessity of a logical story; and another ten percent warned against writing what you wouldn't be interested in reading. I doubt whether anyone would disagree with those particular pieces of advice.

At random, then, I've picked the following nuggets from the MWA gold mine, and a rich lode it is:

ROSS MACDONALD:

The decision on narrative point-of-view is a key one for any novelist. It determines shape and tone, and even the class of detail that can be used.

W. F. NOLAN:

Stay enthused: write what amuses you or angers you or excites you. Then your work will always be fresh — because if *you're* not excited, the reader certainly isn't going to be.

JOSH PACHTER:

Put yourself in your readers' shoes: decide what they will expect you to do next, and then turn around and do something else. In other words, hit 'em where they ain't.

HOWARD BROWNE:

Know your principal characters inside out. That way they'll stay in character in every scene; consequently every scene will play with a true ring to it. Exciting characters make exciting stories; dull characters make wastepaper. You can generate more excitement by having two fascinating people talk in the subway than you can get in a gunfight between tissue-paper characters in the middle of a cyclone.

MARY CRAIG adds to this and says:

The trick I was slowest to learn is the difference it makes in how convincingly you develop minor characters. Principal characters look so much better surrounded by flesh and blood than they do marching around among statues. The time you take on the butcher and the mortician pays off in spades.

MARY BARRETT phrases nicely one of the basic points of technique:

In a good mystery story, the end is tied to the beginning, like a snake putting his tail in his mouth.

JOHN D. MACDONALD:

Always write as if each finished page is the final version, and you will never have another whack at it. If you write with the cozy assumption that you will have a chance to rewrite, then your work will get so loose and sloppy that you will find yourself rewriting with the cozy assumption that you will have a chance to re-rewrite . . .

EARLE N. LORD disagrees, but offers an interesting and unusual suggestion:

I have found it of great value to record my first draft on a tape casette the day after writing the story, then several days or weeks later, to listen to the casette as I read and revise the story. Hearing the story helps to eliminate wrenched and tangled style, repetitions, and rough dialogue.

KATHLEEN S. RICH finds:

There are times when I write and rewrite and still something about a character does not jell; it has been my experience at these times to discover that the problem is simply that I do not *like* being inside this character, having his thoughts, and in a sense I am trying to get around him. A bit of a solution is to hate that villain if you must, yet before you commit him to paper, search for even a small crumb of understanding or compassion. The character will come across much better for it.

JOHN BALL:

To write the first sentence of a book in such a

way as to make the reader want to continue on to the second; to make the first paragraph compel the reading of the second; and to make the first chapter all but force the reading of the second. After that if the reader isn't hooked, the book is a failure.

BRIAN GARFIELD:

There's one trick that always works and doesn't get much press. I don't know quite how to tag it; maybe call it the "Plant it early, pay it off later" trick. In other words, set up a mystery and then give the reader what looks like a solution, and then later on show him another solution to the same mystery.

ROBERT A. LEVEY:

Be perceptive. Be on the watch at all times for the unusual whether you see it or find it in newspapers, magazines, or journals. Clip or write down this information. It is surprising what eventually will be accumulated.

PHYLLIS A. WHITNEY:

To keep interest high make sure that your main character has an immediate purpose in every scene — something he wants to *do* that will carry him into action and possible conflict. If you must have a scene in which he is drifting without a strong purpose, then give another character in the scene something he must act upon to affect your hero.

BAYNARD KENDRICK:

Never write about anybody, any place, or anything that you don't know more about than anyone living — at least in your own estimation.

WILLIAM BRITTAIN:

Try to discover the plot possibilities in everyday

situations — a torn shirt or a drive in the country, for example.

RICHARD S. PRATHER:

Hit him when he's down. Few professionals, but many beginning writers, give in to the temptation to make things easier for their protagonist — because that's easier for the writer. Don't do it. Make things tougher for your hero, get him in deep and then deeper, pile on the troubles, ruin the guy (almost), sock it to him. Hit him when he's down. When nothing else helps, pray. Or get bombed. Then hit again.

RICHARD MARTIN STERN:

Coincidence is all right, it's fine — if it works *against* your hero. Try making it work for him, and you fall flat on your face.

DAN MARLOWE:

Upon completion of a manuscript, assign three pertinent adjectives to each major character. The hero, for instance, might be bold, fearless and scatterbrained. The heroine might be virginal, timid and erudite. The writer should go back and examine each line of dialogue to be certain that the characterization assigned to the individual is reflected in his words. I have found this to be a great tightener.

PATRICK O'KEEFFE:

When seeking an inspiration for a story, read a published one of the kind you want to write.

MARGARET MANNERS:

Research. If you have to get something up, of which you know nothing, first go to the children's library and get a book on the subject there. Read it carefully and make notes. Then you are prepared to tackle the subject on a higher level; at least you will be familiar with the special technical vocabulary. Then, let the character through whose eyes we are seeing the special setting be a person totally unfamiliar with what is going on. That way, any slips you may make are your ignorant character's and not yours, and you've made room for humor.

CARL HENRY RATHJEN:

In book length start with a mystery situation in which you, the author, do not know the solution any more than your main character does.

JOE L. HENSLEY takes sharp issue:

Know what your ending is before you make a beginning.

LAURA W. DOUGLAS:

Don't kill too many good guys — most readers want the bad guys relegated to oblivion. When precious words and delicious phrases muddy the plot, they should be recycled. Eliminate dreams. They bore a reader and are proof that the author is inadequate to deal with the reality of his plot and has to depend on mystique to give a reader a hint and maybe scare him sufficiently to finish the book.

ENID S. RUSSELL:

Mystery fiction has acquired a reputation for poor writing, and the best counsel I can offer is: Learn to write well, write about the things, places, people, milieu you know best, and then edit your work as though it were someone else's.

THOMAS PATRICK McMAHON:

Never, never, never, tell anyone what you're writing. Some of the greatest books in the minds of writers were talked to death. Nobody likes to write — everybody loves to have written.

WILLIAM P. McGIVERN:

To quote Somerset Maugham: "Don't explain overmuch." And to quote the Master, P. G. Wodehouse, re the stage. "Never let anybody sit down in the second act." If a writer looks behind these comments, he will see that they suggest several other wise injunctions.

ROBERT L. FISH:

The best and most important trick of the mystery trade, I think, is not to be afraid to give ample clues. The fact is that 99.99 percent of readers go right past 99.99 percent of most clues without seeing them. The same is true of editors. Basically, I think both the reader and the editor *want* to be mystified. If the plot is strong, give all the clues you want. It will make the book better, not easier, for the reader.

WILLIAM T. BRANNON:

Read the work of other writers. Read something every day.

HAROLD Q. MASUR:

Reading halfway through a book, then trying to solve the problem on my own. If I am wrong, I then have a new solution, probably a new villain, and these can be used as plotting devices for starting a new story.

NANCY SCHACHTERLE:

I've learned that my characters must be *real.* I make notes of interesting faces on TV, not only recording their physical appearance but also what of the character comes through, and why and how. In church, in restaurants, even at private gatherings, I notice facial expressions, gestures, and visible temperament, making notes when I can.

ARTHUR MALING:

I try to follow the advice that has been attributed to Hemingway. When you quit for the day, try to quit in the middle of a sentence. At least it gives you something to start with the next day.

MIRIAM LYNCH and ELISABETH OGILVIE offer advice along the same lines. MIRIAM LYNCH:

I think that if you leave the manuscript, not because it is not moving well, but rather because you know what you are going to do in the next few pages, it will give you an eagerness to return to the writing. If you are developing a "writer's block," destroy your last few pages and start again at a point where you are satisfied with what you have done so far. Tension and worry breed a stronger dose of the same.

ELISABETH OGILVIE:

Never finish a chapter or a section at the end of a working day. Or if you finish toward the end of a session, start the next part immediately, even if it's only a paragraph, and you break off in the middle of a sentence.

TIFFANY HOLMES:

Don't force it. If it isn't flowing onto the page, do something else. Put it on a back burner and don't touch it till it boils over, and don't listen to too many chefs' cooking advice.

ERIC AMBLER:

For me, the way to salvation has always been thorough rewriting, or, when that hasn't worked, through discarding. The latter process may be painful, but when it's over the effects can be constructively exhilarating.

When JANET GREGORY VERMANDEL has plot trouble, she has a unique way of handling it:

The Vermandel sure cure for plot-holes — Solitaire. Wordless, mindless pastime that keeps my hands busy while my mind rolls free. I play Solitaire blindly, by the hour, stopping only to scribble off pages of plot, as ideas swim up from my subconscious. Works like a charm time after time, and takes the curse off plotting. At all other times, I despise Solitaire.

DANA LYON has this pearl:

Something that I learned long ago: when the book starts to bog down in the middle, *make something happen!* Footsteps in the night? No matter whose, bring them in and work them out later. The love story is getting dull? Bring in a godawful fight with a climax that will make the reader wonder if these two can ever get together again. The detective can't quite make it? Okay, turn him around and let him be the villain, and the villain the detective. More darn fun. I did it with one of my books and surprised even myself.

And finally, JOE GORES, sums it all up when he quotes the advice given to him when he asked a Notre Dame professor how to be a writer:

It's very easy to be a writer. Go to a big city and get a little room with a table and a chair in it. Put your typewriter on the table and your backside on the chair. Start writing. When you stand up ten years later, you'll be a writer.

Index

Other Useful Publications for Writers

Writer's Market, edited by Jane Koester and Paula Arnett Sandhage. The freelancer's bible, containing 4,095 listings covering 8,577 paying markets. You'll learn the name and address of the publication, the name of the editor, the kind of material he wants and how much he'll pay to get it. Extra: "How to Break In," a new section in which the editor gives you tips on how to sell to his publication. 896 pp. $13.50.

Writing and Selling Science Fiction, edited by C. L. Grant. A knowledgeable handbook to an exciting but oft-misunderstood genre. Eleven articles by top-flight sf writers on markets, characters, dialogue, "crazy" ideas, world-building, alien-building, money and more. 256 pp. $7.95.

The Craft of Interviewing, by John Brady. Everything you always wanted to know about asking questions, but were afraid to ask — from an experienced interviewer and editor of *Writer's Digest*. The most comprehensive guide to interviewing on the market. 256 pp. $7.95.

A Guide to Writing History, by Doris Ricker Marston. How to track down Big Foot, or your family Civil War letters, or your hometown's last century, for publication and profit. Where to find pictures and illustrations. How to prepare a manuscript for publication. A timely handbook for history buffs and writers. 258 pp. $8.50.

The Confession Writer's Handbook, by Florence K. Palmer. A stylish and informative guide to getting started and getting ahead in the confessions. Palmer, a veteran confessor, discusses the problems of confessions — and their solutions — as if she were sitting across the kitchen table from you. How to start a confession and carry it through. How to take an insignificant event and make it significant. 171 pp. $6.95.

A Complete Guide to Marketing Magazine Articles, by Duane Newcomb. "Anyone who can write a clear sentence can learn to write and sell articles on a consistent basis," says Newcomb (who has published well over 3,000 articles). Here's how. 248 pp. $6.95.

The Creative Writer, edited by Aron Mathieu. This book opens the door to the real world of publishing. Packed with inspiration, techniques, and ideas for writers. Plus inside tips from Maugham, Caldwell, Purdy and others. 416 pp. $6.95.

Handbook of Short Story Writing, edited by Frank A. Dickson and Sandra Smythe. You provide the pencil, paper, and sweat — and this book will provide the expert guidance. Features include James Hilton (*Good-bye, Mr. Chips*) on creating a lovable character; R. V. Cassill, novelist and teacher of writing, on plotting a short story. 238 pp. $6.95.

A Treasury of Tips for Writers, edited by Marvin Weisbord. Features everything from Vance Packard's system of organizing notes, to tips on how to get your research done free. From 86 professional magazine writers. 174 pp. $5.95.

One Way to Write Your Novel, by Dick Perry. For Perry, a novel is 200 pages. Or, two pages a day for 100 days. Then he starts his next novel. And you can start — and finish — *your* novel, with the help of this step-by-step guide taking you from the blank sheet to the polished page. 138 pp. $6.95.

The Poet and the Poem, by Judson Jerome. A rare journey into the night of the poem — the mechanics, the mystery, the craft and sullen art. Written by the most widely read authority on poetry in America, and a major contemporary poet in his own right. 482 pp. $7.95 ($6.95 paperback).

Writing and Selling Non-Fiction, by Hayes B. Jacobs. A durable and frank guide, by a writer who has appeared in *The New Yorker, Harper's* and *Esquire.* Explores with style and know-how the book market, organization and research, finding new markets, interviewing, humor, agents, writer's fatigue and more. One of the leading books of its kind. 317 pp. $7.95.

The Beginning Writer's Answer Book, edited by Kirk Polking and Jean Chimsky. "What is a query letter?" "If I use a pen name, how can I cash the check?" These are among 500 questions most frequently asked by beginning writers — and expertly answered in this down-to-earth handbook. Cross-indexed. 168 pp. $5.95.

Writing Popular Fiction, by Dean R. Koontz. How to write mysteries, suspense thrillers, science fiction, Gothic romances, adult fantasy, Westerns and erotica. The difference between a Big Sexy Novel and a Rough Sexy Novel, and where the fortune is. Here's an inside guide to lively fiction, by a lively novelist. 232 pp. $7.95.

Writing for Children and Teenagers, by Lee Wyndham. Author of over 50 children's books shares her secrets for selling to this large, lucrative market. Features: the 12-point recipe for plotting, and the ten commandments for writers. 253 pp. $8.95.

Artist's and Photographer's Market, edited by Lynne Lapin, Kirk Polking and Paula Arnett Sandhage. Contains 3,667 listings covering 9,168 paying markets for illustrations, photography, designs, cartoons, crafts, and fine arts. Puts the freelance artist right in the picture with cameo interviews, a glossary of art terms, and an ABC of original graphics. 736 pp. $10.95.

The Cartoonist's and Gag Writer's Handbook, by Jack Markow. Longtime cartoonist with thousands of sales reveals the secrets of successful cartooning — step by step. Richly illustrated. 159 pp. $7.95.

The Greeting Card Writer's Handbook, by H. Joseph Chadwick. A complete guide to a near half-million-dollar market. A former greeting card editor tells you what editors look for in inspirational verse . . . how to write humor . . . what to write about for conventional, studio and juvenile cards. Extra: a renewable list of greeting card markets. Will be greeted by any freelancer. 268 pp. $6.95.

Writer's Digest. The world's leading magazine for writers. Monthly issues include timely articles, interviews, columns, tips to keep writers informed on where and how to sell their work. One year subscription, $12.

(Prices subject to change without notice.)
Writer's Digest, 9933 Alliance Road, Cincinnati, Ohio 45242.